COMPOSING AT THE KEYBOARD WITH THE

MUSICARTA EASY PIANO STYLE

R A Chappell

Pieces with thirds

(continued over)

MUSICARTA PUBLICATIONS

ISBN: 978-0-620-61072-8

(continued)

Pieces with sixths

Introduction

The Musicarta Easy Piano Style (MEPS) course of lessons provides a methodical approach to developing a creative modern keyboard playing style. The MEPS approach is to show players which notes on the keyboard will go together and to teach attractive, rhythmic textures for playing them.

The MEPS style of learning is an introduction to 'composing at the keyboard', and invites keyboard players to think of themselves as creators of music, not just reproducers. Each module in the workbook adds a new aspect to your ability to find music in the keyboard, showing you what to play and how to practice it.

MEPS modules teach an easy way of playing chords from chord symbols in other musical circumstances, and the lessons provide an opportunity for learning about harmony and developing your musical ear.

The volume you are holding is the print-only version of the MEPS course book from CreateSpace/Amazon Books. The print-your-own version, which includes MIDI and audio music example files, is available only directly from www.musicarta.com.

Good-to-intermediate readers will find the print-only workbook quite adequate, but less practised readers might want to invest in the supplementary audio download available from Musicarta.

Modern keyboard styling is heavily syncopated and requires a particular teaching approach. The MEPS download includes audio files for all the studies and progressive build-up examples, and the module studies and pieces have video counterparts on the MisterMusicarta YouTube channel, so learners can watch a performance and get an overall view of the hand patterning they are aiming for.

Also included in the download are all the example and study/piece MIDI files, and the MidiPiano virtual keyboard to play them on, offering another non-manuscript performance guide. Taken together, these three parallel resources offer even elementary readers a good chance of learning all the studies and pieces – and, more importantly, of understanding how the music is being created right at the keyboard.

Videos of the main module performances are however publicly available to all on the Mister Musicarta YouTube MEPS playlist. The video URLs are printed at the back of the book.

The audio files

Nearly every musical example in the MEPS workbook has associated audio and MIDI files. These are shown in the tables below the written-out music. If the example has an associated video (on the MisterMusicarta YouTube MEPS playlist), this is referenced in the right hand table cell.

FPOC_01	(Video)

As an aid to learning the audio files for the build-up examples are in most cases edited to 'loop' (repeat constantly) with your media player's 'Repeat' function active. For a more accurate repeat function and greater versatility, try using 'Audacity', a simple, reliable sound editor which can loop audio tracks seamlessly.

The MIDI files

The file numbering for the example audio and MIDI files is the same. You will soon recognise the different icons your operating system uses for the two types of file. Most operating system will play the MIDI file as a basic audio file using a simple on-board synthesiser.

Also included in the supplementary download is the MidiPiano virtual keyboard. MidiPiano can be seen in action on most of the YouTube MEPS videos. Its piano roll pane, repeat, speed and key functions make it an invaluable learning tool.

MIDI files are simple to play on MidiPiano – you launch MidiPiano and use the application Open command to load the file. You are strongly advised to make friends with MidiPiano – it is an invaluable learning aid. ('Synthesia' is a good non-Windows alternative) See the Musicarta 'MidiPiano' web page for full instructions.

Module audio and MIDI files have a code (FPOC for First Pair of Chords, for example) which is shown in the module title block. Audio and MIDI files for learning segments and exercises have the same name. Your operating system will assign them different icons, and if you 'sort by type', they will arrange themselves in separate lists. Main performances have fuller, more descriptive titles.

Leave the audio and MIDI files in the folders they come in, but unpack the enclosing folder if convenient.

Preparing to learn

A little time spent become adept at accessing and playing the audio, MIDI and video resources and arranging your working environment so you can control playback at your piano keyboard will pay dividends in quicker progress.

You will also make speedier progress if you listen to the MEPS audio material repeatedly away from the keyboard – by arranging the MEPS performance mp3s in order on your audio listening device, for example.

What is Musicarta?

Musicarta – the www.musicarta.com website, Musicarta Publications and the MisterMusicarta YouTube channel – is dedicated to teaching musical creativity at the keyboard through a combination of usable music theory, easily grasped keyboard textures (chord-tone patterns) and coached modern syncopation skills.

Please note that all Musicarta publications material is copyright. Please respect intellectual property and only reproduce the material for commonly agreed 'fair use' study purposes.

The First Pair of Chords (FPOC)

In this first module, you learn the Musicarta Easy Piano Style (MEPS) hand position and see how you can easily make music on just two chords – with a few added 'next-door notes' and an attractive modern rhythm texture.

Here are the audio/MID/video references files for this module's final performance.

| FPOC perf | (Video) |

Placing the left hand

The MEPS left hand plays the root, fifth and octave notes of the chord. Copy the illustration below to find the MEPS left hand position for a C major chord.

- Put your left hand little finger (LH5) on a C (= root).
- Put your thumb (LH1) on the next C up (= octave – also a root note).
- Your second finger (LH2) will very likely be right over the fifth (G). Check by counting white keys one up to five starting from C = 1.

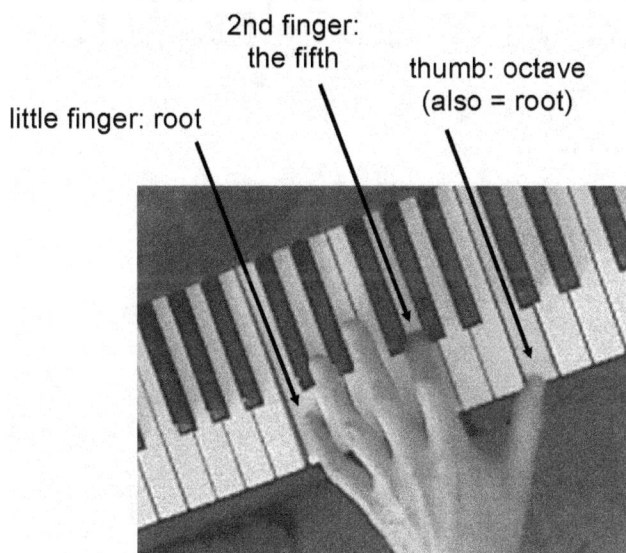

2nd finger: the fifth

thumb: octave (also = root)

little finger: root

(To match up with the music below, your thumb will need to be on 'middle C' on your keyboard.)

The standard MEPS left hand position

The basic left hand pattern is an up-and-down rocking movement, playing bottom-middle-top-middle (B, M, T, M) notes over and over.

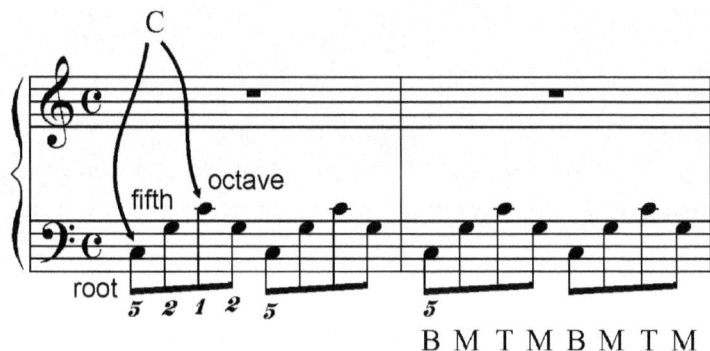

| FPOC_02 |

B M T M B M T M

(If you thumb is on middle C, the music and the hand in the photo will match up.)

Both LH5 and LH1 (the left hand little finger and thumb) play the note named in the chord symbol. (Musicarta sometimes calls the root the 'name-note'.) This makes the Musicarta Easy Piano Style a great introduction to playing music from chord charts and sheet music.

What the right hand does

The three notes of the MEPS left hand texture are easy to find, but, on their own, they sound rather 'bald', because they lack one of the three essential chord tones – the third. The third therefore features prominently in the right hand as the melody note, usually played together with the first of the four left hand quavers.

Here is the left hand pattern on its own, then with the right hand thirds added in.

FPOC_03

But the right hand (melody) can't be confined to the third only! Here are the thirds in the right hand again, then with the next-door notes played in between.

FPOC_04

Build-up of syncopation

For some rhythmic variety, move the in-between note onto the fourth quaver of the group.

Modern popular music very often plays notes 'off the beat'. This is not usually easy for beginners, to start with. Play your MIDI or audio file on repeat and be prepared to keep going until the shifted notes feel natural – and you can come back and find the performance again easily.

FPOC_05

Now practice moving that melody 'wobble' forward one quaver.

FPOC_06

Here's a one-line study combining those rhythms

FPOC_07

The same build-up in D minor

If you move both hands one piano key to the right, you can generate the same music in D minor. The repetitions in the build-up have been reduced, and note also that you use RH3 (right hand middle finger) on the F note (the third).

Dm

the right hand thirds · thirds and next-door notes

The left hand pattern

next-door notes moved to the fourth quaver · the melody 'wobble' pulled forward

the combination riff

FPOC_08

Combining the two positions

We can make a short piece of music using these two chord positions (C and D minor). Here is a practice segment that oscillates between the two positions.

C · Dm

FPOC_09

Repeat the line until you're comfortable with it.

We're going to make moving between the C and D minor chords a little more interesting. Here is the un-syncopated 'base' music of the changing-position pattern we'll be developing.

FPOC_10

Now here is the same music with some syncopation and a rest between movements.

FPOC_11

As soon as you can, progress to a version without the long rest between positions.

FPOC_12

If you find you're getting stuck, one good technique is to play the MIDI file on MidiPiano with the Repeat function on, slow it down if necessary, and play along on an imaginary keyboard away from the actual keyboard until you've got the finger pattern ("what goes with what") right. Then go to your keyboard and try it again

The completed study

The music for the completed module study (as in the module video) is on the next page.

MEPS: Pairs of Chords - C and D minor

Here's a slightly simpler version, without the right hand joining-up notes.

FPOC_13

It's nice to come away from a practice session with some kind of completed performance. Musicarta calls these 'stepping stone' performances, or versions.

A build-up practice video

On the following pages you will find the MS for a full straight-through first-pair build-up shown in this video.

(Video)

This can be your model for how to practice any syncopated riff. You build up from simple to more complicated, and not just once, but over and over again, to build a firm foundation for your modern Keyboard style. .

The video ends with a performance of the module study.

Build-up of syncoaption in C

C   Thirds in the right hand

The left hand pattern

Thirds and next-door notes   Next-door notes moved to the fourth quaver

The last melody 'wobble' pulled forward   The final combination pattern

Condensed build-up of syncopation in D minor

Dm   Thirds in the right hand   Thirds and next-door notes

The left hand pattern

Next-door notes moved to the fourth quaver   The last melody 'wobble' pulled forward

The final combination pattern

The pattern in C and D minor

Joining-up notes, without syncopation

Joining-up, syncopated, one direction at a time.

Joining up, syncopated, continuous

A Second Pair of Chords (SPOC)

Like the first module, this module uses the MEPS hand position and rhythmic textures on just two chords to make a piece of music. Again, they are next-door chords – this time, E minor and D major, and the higher chord (E minor) is the home chord. The music in this module therefore has the E minor key signature, which is F sharp.

Source the module audio/MID/video references files and find your E minor and D hand positions in the Visual Glossary on p.28 (non-readers) or just copy the video.

SPOC perf	(Video)

The video demonstrates the four stages of the rhythmic (syncopated) development.

Here is the base material – the standard eight-quaver left hand with the right hand melody 'wobbling' around the third (chord tone).

SPOC_02

A slight adjustment moves the emphasis in the even-numbered bars onto the notes either side of the third (the fourth and second).

SPOC_03

Next, we are going to pull forward most of the right hand notes. This is called 'anticipation' – you anticipate the notes, play them early. (This is the video Section 1.)

SPOC_04

Counting

To understand properly what we're doing, we have to look at 'the counts'. A bar of four-four (as here) has four crotchets in a bar, counted "One, two, three, four".

SPOC_02

Note that the counting in the example above applies to the right hand (treble clef, melody), so where there isn't a note, the count is in brackets (it would be whispered, if you are counting out loud).

The quavers between the main crotchet beats (when there is one) are counted "and", indicated in the music by the ampersand (&). Here's a made-up example.

SPOC_05

So the count of our anticipated version is:

SPOC_04

The right hand only plays on the beat at the start of a bar. The rest of the notes are 'off the beat' – on the 'ands'.

Left hand finger 2 plays the off-beat quavers, so right hand off-the-beat notes come with LH2 (as indicated in the fingering). This is a good way of making sure you play off-the-beat right hand notes in the right place.

Module Study, first version

You already have enough material now for the simplest version of the module study. This is 'Section 1' of the module video.

Notes to the last line of music

- Both hands are claiming the middle E. The right hand plays it as a melody note (end of line two), then surrenders it for the left hand pattern (indicated by the little pair of brackets). In fact, it's held by the sustain pedal ('Ped.'), but it's still thought of as a melody note.

- In the first two bars of the last line, the left hand 'drops' quavers again – this time, quavers 4 and 5 on counts "(2) and 3". This pattern forms the basis of the next version of this study.

- In the Musicarta Easy Piano Style, the kind of ending used in line 3 is called a 'ladder' – the hands combined pass the music up through a series of roots (E) and fifths (B). The beaming in bar 11 indicates the pattern being passed up from the left hand (bass clef) into the right (treble clef).

The second version

The second version of the module study is an exercise in two-handed syncopation. The left hand plays its dropped-quaver variant while the right hand stays exactly the same. Look-and-listen to the performance first.

This pattern is shown in Section 2 of the module video.

SPOC_07

Further help: Together, left, right analysis

It's only a small development but, now that the left hand has gaps, you will probably have to slow it right down and work out, count by count, which right hand notes go with which left hand notes.

Musicarta calls this ultra-close examination of the sequence of events, 'together-left-right (TLR) analysis'. Look at our typical two-bar pattern.

SPOC_08

(The audio/MIDI repeats the pattern at practice speed.)

Note that the count now takes both hands into account, and tied (held) notes only count when they are played.

The sequence of events is:

$$T\ T\ L\ R\ (\ )\ T\ L\ T\ |\ T\ T\ L\ R\ (\ )\ T\ L\ L$$

Only one 'quaver slot' is empty – the fifth one, on count 3.

It's a good practice technique to learn to 'tap' this two-handed rhythm away from the keyboard first – on a table top, for example. You can use your left hand fingers 5, 2, 1 in their proper order while your right hand taps the melody rhythm.

Using the MIDI file and MidiPiano – or any other virtual keyboard – you can see the actual sequence of events and tap along until you're ready to go to play the real thing at the keyboard.

The 'smoothed rhythm' version (optional)

To 'smooth' the right hand rhythm – as in the actual module performance – we take quaver-and-crotchet pairs, add their time value together and split it into two equal notes (dotted quavers).

To practice this effect, we are going to revert temporarily to our all-eight-quaver left hand. Here's the usual (syncopated) two-handed pattern with the selected pairs circled.

SPOC_09

Here is the smoothing effect applied, still with the all-quaver left hand.

SPOC_10

This pattern is demonstrated in Section 3 of the module video. The right hand notes that come between the left hand quavers have the dashed lines dropping down to indicate between which left hand quavers they actually fall. All the other right hand notes come with left hand quavers.

Now here is the smoothed right hand with the dropped-quaver left hand.

SPOC_11

MEPS: Pairs of Chords - E minor and D

Only the circled right hand notes are affected by the change in the left hand pattern – they now come on their own. This pattern is shown in Section 4 of the module video.

Here is the audio/MIDI reference for the last three examples combined, using both the E minor and D major hand positions. The MS for the finished study is on the previous page.

$$\boxed{\text{SPOC\_12}}$$

Remember that the rhythmic 'smoothing' is a performance development you can leave to be acquired over time. The study sounds fine with the original crotchet-and-quaver right hand combination – just make sure to end the study artistically, every time.

MEPS Hand Positions

The MEPS hand position is an excellent way to quickly start making music at the keyboard. Take time to get to know how to find it, and to understand how and why it works.

(Note that this is a reference section. It is not necessary for you to work through this section thoroughly at this point. You can, if you like, skim and make a mental note of the contents for a later re-visit and move straight on to the next music making module. You can also skip forward to page 27 for a collection of MEPS hand position graphics.)

The MEPS left hand position

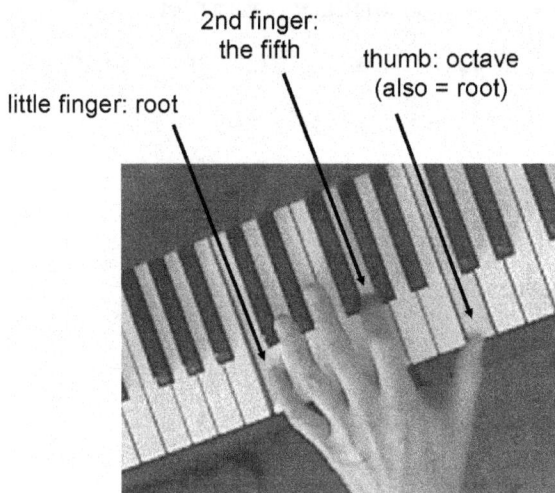

The standard MEPS left hand position

R stands for 'root' – the note named in the chord symbol – and '8' (the octave) is the root note also. The left hand plays the root, fifth and octave (R, 5, 8) and the right plays the third (3). Note that these numbers are chords tones and not fingering numbers.

Counting the MEPS hand position

If the root R is any white piano key other than B, you can simply count up five white keys from the root (with the root as "one") to find your fifth (5).

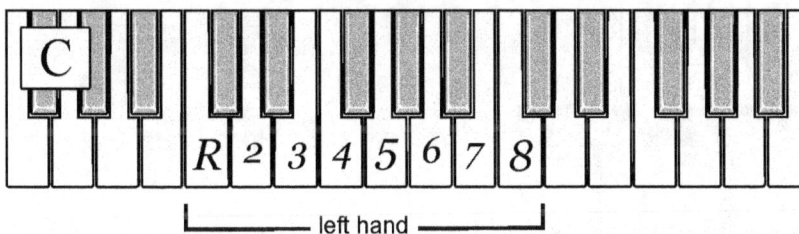

The other way to verify the fifth is to count up seven semitones from the root. Note that semitones in music are counted from zero (R = 0). This is the only reliable way to find the fifth where the root is a black key or white-key B.

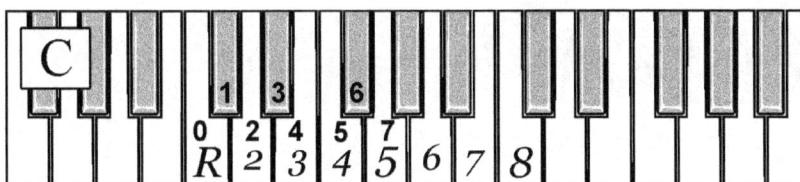

If you put your left little finger (LH5) and your left thumb (LH1) on notes named in the chord symbol (roots, the 'name-note'), your left hand index finger (LH2) will probably fall over the fifth anyway – as shown in the photo above.

The right hand – finding the third

The left hand plays the root and fifth. On their own, these two notes do not make a satisfactory chord. There is one chord tone missing – the third – still to be found.

Scale tones are counted from 1 in music, so the octave, 8 – the same note as the root – is also 1 of the next octave. But it's actually only safe to count up to the third (from the root or octave) in semitones because the third is in a different place in minor as compared with major chords.

Unlike scale tones, semitones are counted from zero – like measuring with a ruler.

If the chord is major (C, D etc. – single capital letters only), the third is four semitones above the octave/root.

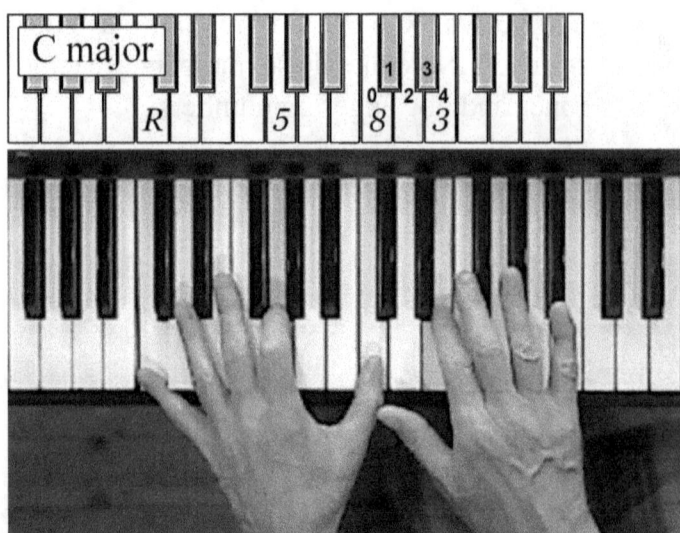

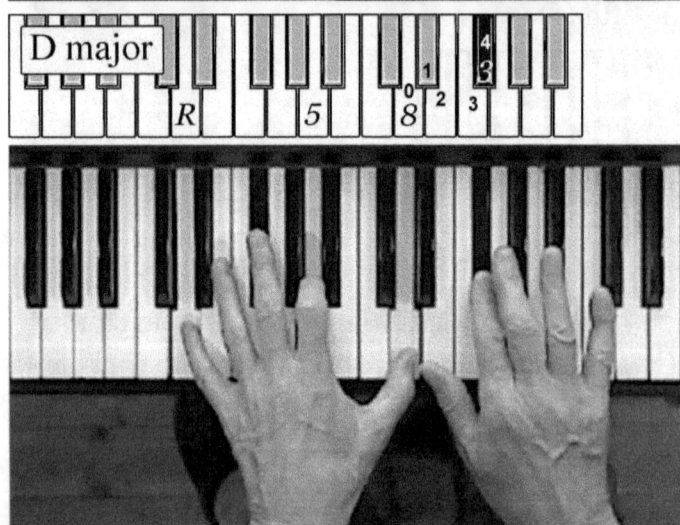

Note that any right hand finger might be used to play the third.

If the chord is minor (Dm, Am – for D minor, A minor etc.), the third is only three semitones above the root.

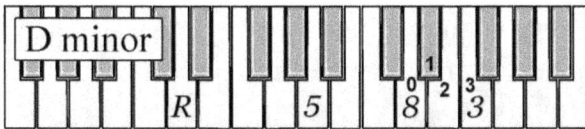

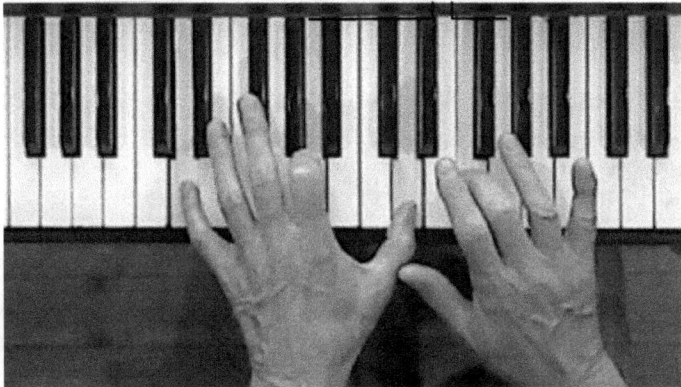

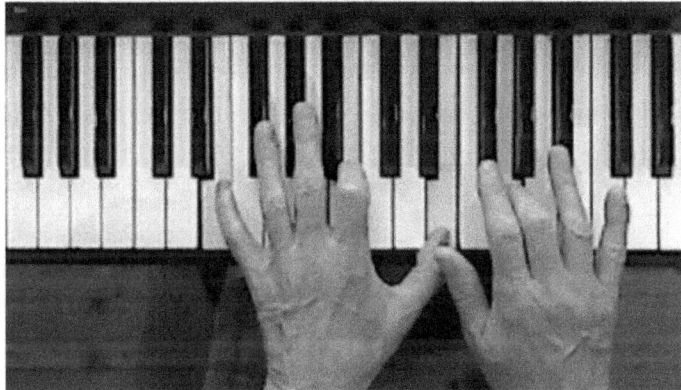

The basic MEPS rhythmic texture

In the Musicarta Easy Piano Style, the left hand usually just rocks from side to side, playing its three notes (root, fifth, octave) in quavers in a simple bottom, middle, top, middle (B, M, T, M) sequence.

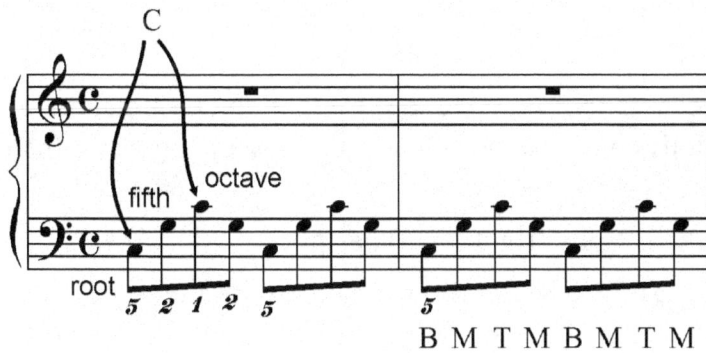

FPOC_0
2

The simplest MEPS left hand pattern has a note on every quaver beat. We say, "All the quavers 'slots' are filled." (In more advanced MEPS left hand patterns, some of the quavers are not played – we say they are "dropped".)

Counting the left hand

One advantage of the MEPS left hand texture – especially when you come to play syncopated, off-the-beat right hand material – is that you can easily use it to find 'the counts'

Nearly always, the left hand little finger and thumb (LH5 and LH1) play 'on the beat' – on counts 1, 2, 3, 4 etc. The middle left hand note (LH2) comes on the off-beat 'and'.

So any off-the-beat, syncopated melody (right hand) notes – those on '&' in the example below – will come at the same time as LH2, not with the little finger or thumb.

SPOC_04

This is a big help in working out which notes come together and playing off-the-beat notes.

Shared notes

The MEPS hand position usually puts the essential 'third' (chord tone) in the right hand, but from time to time the right hand (the melody) will also use the root – the same note that the left hand thumb needs to play its 'octave' note.

When the hands have to share any note, the melody (right hand) has priority.

Often the left hand will play the shared note and then surrender it quickly for the right hand to use. Sometimes, the left hand will not play the note at all – but it will still appear in the left hand music as part of the accompaniment. In both cases, a small pair of brackets appears in the music to bring the matter to your attention.

Usually, the sustain pedal will be used to 'gloss over' the difficulty.

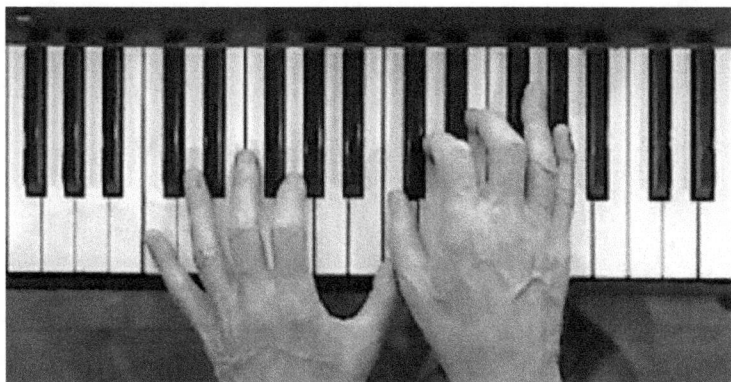

Although your hands are sharing a note, they shouldn't have to fight over the space! Usually, you push your right hand further back down the keys so it's more 'over' your left hand. The picture below shows the thumbs sharing the middle C note. Watch the videos closely to see how to 'manage' your hands at these points.

Visual glossary of hand positions

The chords/hand positions are shown in the order they appear in the workbook. Note that the notes shown could be higher or lower on the keyboard.

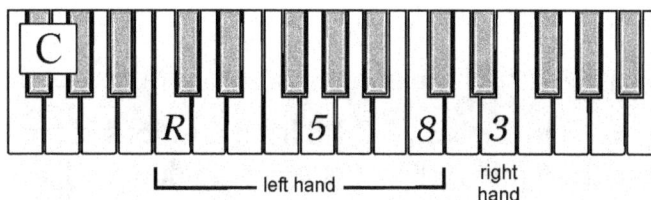

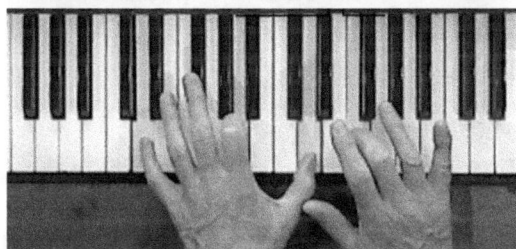

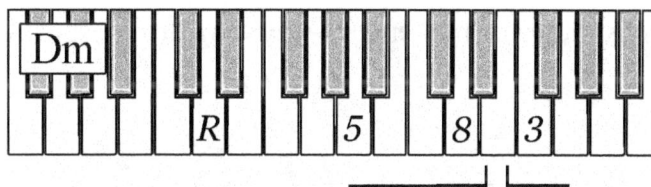

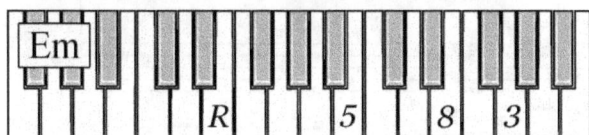

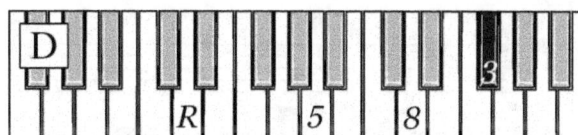

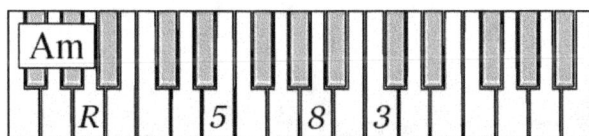

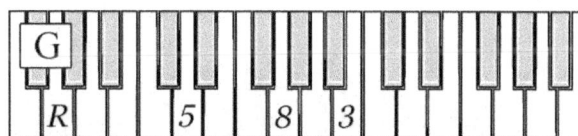

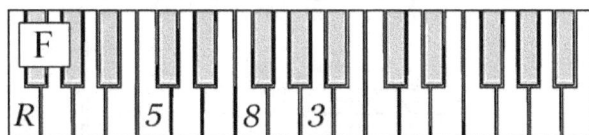

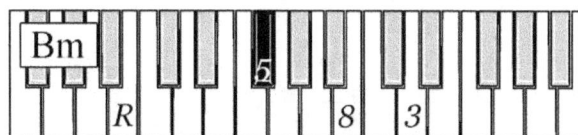

This collection of chord/hand positions covers all the workbook material through to the 'Introducing Thirds' module on page 49.

One Fourth and a Pair (OFAP)

The previous modules in this workbook have explored two pairs of chords using the Musicarta Easy Piano Style. This module uses exactly the same principles to produce a keyboard composition covering three positions (chords): A minor, E minor and D major. A minor and E minor are a fourth apart, hence the title.

The final-version module study is called *The Vigil*, and is a series of variations on the basic fourth-plus-a-pair movement (MS at end of module). Here is what it sounds like.

| OFAP perf | (Video) |

The chord sequence for the music you've just heard is:

1

Am	Em	Am	Em	Am	Em	D	Em

33   *(repeats)*

D	Em	D	D	Em	Em

The basic eight-chord phrase plays four times before going on to the extended ending at bar 33.

You can find the basic MEPS hand positions in the glossary on page 27. Note that both hands play in the treble clef, that is, above middle C. The music is in E minor – key signature, F sharp.

Movement and variations

Here is the basic movement – walking down from A minor to E minor and back again

OFAP_02

The left hand stops on count 3, when the right hand walks to the third of the next chord.

Now, introduce some anticipation in the right hand. The left hand plays one fewer quavers.

OFAP_03

Extend the right hand run as far as the root of the E minor chord, and carry the pattern over into the D major bar.

Here's the same right hand with a different left hand.

One more right hand note is anticipated – the melody C in bar 3 is brought forward into the end of bar 2. The counting applies to both hands combined.

Competing notes

The hands play close together in the Musicarta Easy Piano Style, and in fact they often compete over the same note, (usually the root) which is needed both as a melody note and in the rhythmic left hand pattern (ostinato). This is indicated in the MS by a small pair of brackets which say, in effect, "Get out of the way quickly – this note will soon be needed by your other hand!"

To achieve this effect, you play the first of the two notes very short but use the sustain pedal so it doesn't sound staccato. It may take a little time to master playing like this. There's an easier left hand which skirts round the problem – and is actually used in the performance of this module's final-version study. You see it in the first bar, below.

You play just five notes – B, M, T, M, B. You can substitute this left hand pattern wherever you find sharing notes too difficult – the important thing is to keep playing.

Development (continued)

Here, the right hand has brought the note D above the A minor third into play.

OFAP_06

Still, count 3 (the fifth quaver) is the only quaver slot where nothing is played. Here are two bars of that pattern with counts and full TLR (together, left, right) analysis.

Repeat the segment until your performance is secure.

OFAP_07

Rhythmic smoothing

Now here is the right hand rhythmically 'smoothed' as in previous modules.

OFAP_08

The first two-bar pattern has the dotted lines and counts to show exactly where the in-between right hand notes fall. All the other right hand notes are in the same place as before.

Once you've mastered the smoothed rhythm, you can apply it to any of the patterns. Remember that this rhythmic smoothing is optional. Your performance will sound fine with the original crotchet-plus-quaver pairs.

Melodic 'contour'

Being aware of melodic contour – and deliberately varying it – is an important part of the improviser's skill. (By 'contour', we mean whether the melody goes up or down or stays the same.)

Here's the last line of the previous study with a different up/down contour.

OFAP_09

(Notes continue after the MS.)

The Vigil

R A Chappell

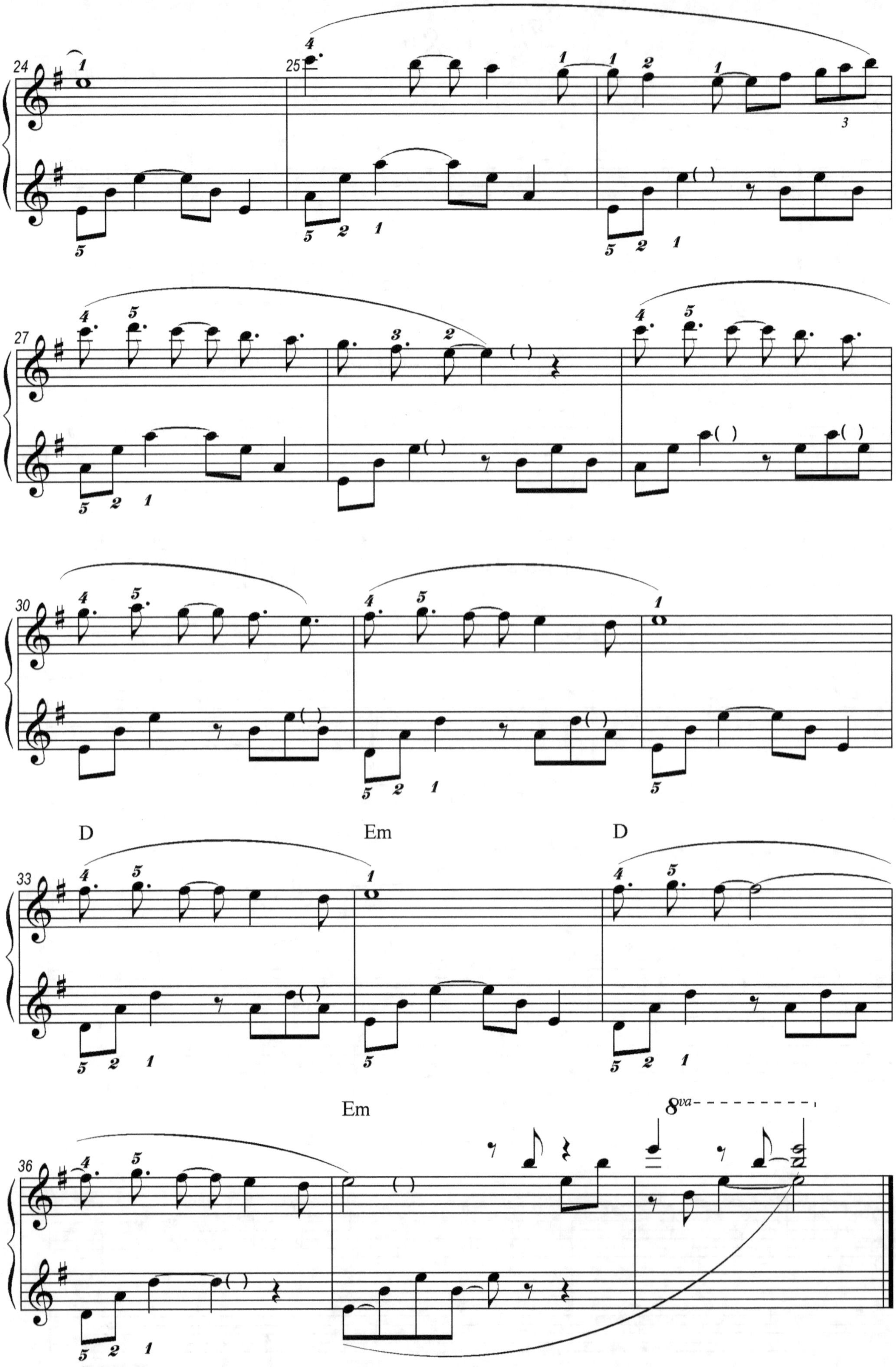
D
Em
D
Em
8va

Here's another melodic contour variation.

$$\boxed{\text{OFAP\_10}}$$

Play this segment on repeat and listen to it carefully until you can hear the up/down pattern and point out where it varies from the previous one. (This is an invaluable exercise in 'playing by ear'.)

Feel free to experiment with the up/down choices and see if you come up with a combination you prefer.

Module performance – *The Vigil*

Here's the finished module study again.

$$\boxed{\text{OFAP\_perf}}\ \boxed{\text{(Video)}}$$

If you listen carefully, you will hear that, in the repeat of the first section, the right hand in bars 10 and 12 has the 'smoothed' rhythm. Tiny variations in repeated material keep it sounding fresh, and often creep into performance by themselves, as your understanding of the music deepens.

Three Fourths and a Pair   (TFAP)

The previous module in this workbook is called 'One Fourth and a Pair' because the chords in its chord sequence are A minor, E minor and D. A minor and E minor are 'the fourth' (the roots are a fourth apart), and E minor and D (major) are the pair.

In harmony, this root-falling-a-fourth is a powerful and much-used dynamic. The study in this module uses three interlocking root-falling-a-fourth pairs. The pairs overlap by one scale tone.

Here are the module audio/MIDI file reference and the chord sequence chart. The chord chart only shows the main repeating phrase in order to show its construction. There's an extended ending, as in the last module study.

TFAP_perf	(Video)

Am	Em	F	C	Dm	Am	G	Am
falling a 4th		falling a 4th		falling a 4th		the tone-apart pair	
	one-note overlap		one-note overlap				

Here is the 'skeleton music' of the piece.

TFAP_02

Looking into a piece to see its 'skeleton music' – and then rehearsing it – is a valuable and time-saving study technique, which you will use from here on in the workbook.

Now you will start developing this 'bare bones' version, using all the techniques from the previous modules. Here's one possible first stage.

TFAP_03

You see that the new material has already inspired a left-hand variation in bars 2 and 4, where quaver 7 (only – on count 4) is dropped.

Next will come the right hand syncopation. Expect the left hand to adapt to the new fall of notes.

TFAP_04

Now run the right hand down to the root of the second chord in each pair.

TFAP_05

Notice the different, in-pairs left hand (first line only). The count and TLR (together, left, right) analysis has been written in, chiefly as a reminder to go through this process in your head whenever you see complicated, syncopated rhythms like this.

To prepare for a final version, practice running up to the first melody note of the next pair, itself anticipated. Use the left hand from the previous version.

TFAP_06

The Musicarta Easy Piano Style is an open-ended formula for creating music at the keyboard. The 'final' version given here is only a suggestion. The main eight-bar phrase repeats – with slight variations each time to keep the music interesting – and the variation suggested just now could be part of your own 'final version'..

Read the chord chart as you listen to the performance. The study starts with a simple 'statement of the theme', and then there are three variations before the extended ending.

TFAP_perf (Video)

1, 9, 17, 25

Am	Em	F	C	Dm	Am	G	Am

33 - Extended ending

Dm	Am	G	G	Am	Am	Am	Am

MEPS: Three Fourths and a Pair

R A Chappell

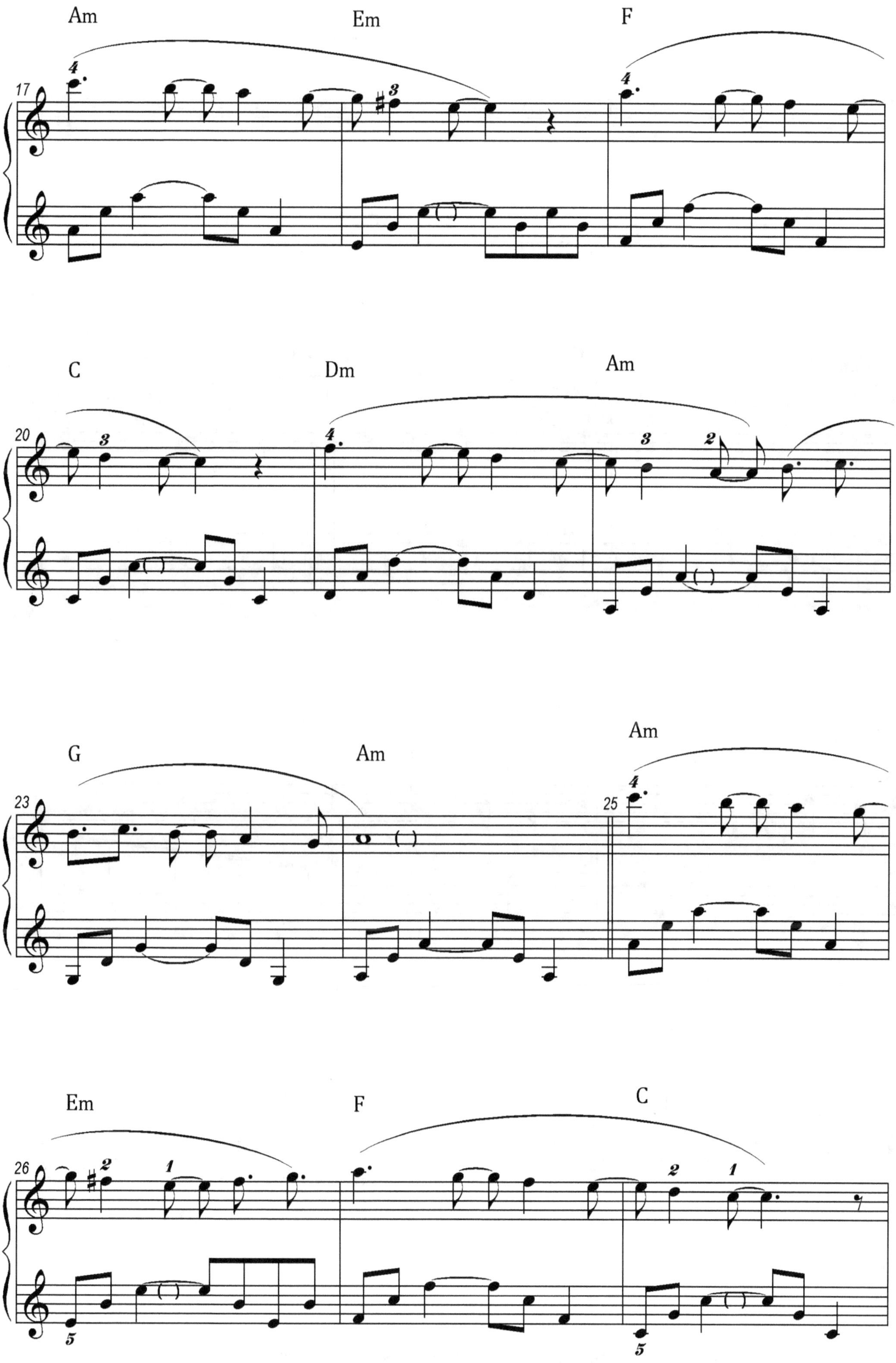

Am
Em
F
C
Dm
Am
G
Am
Am
Em
F
C

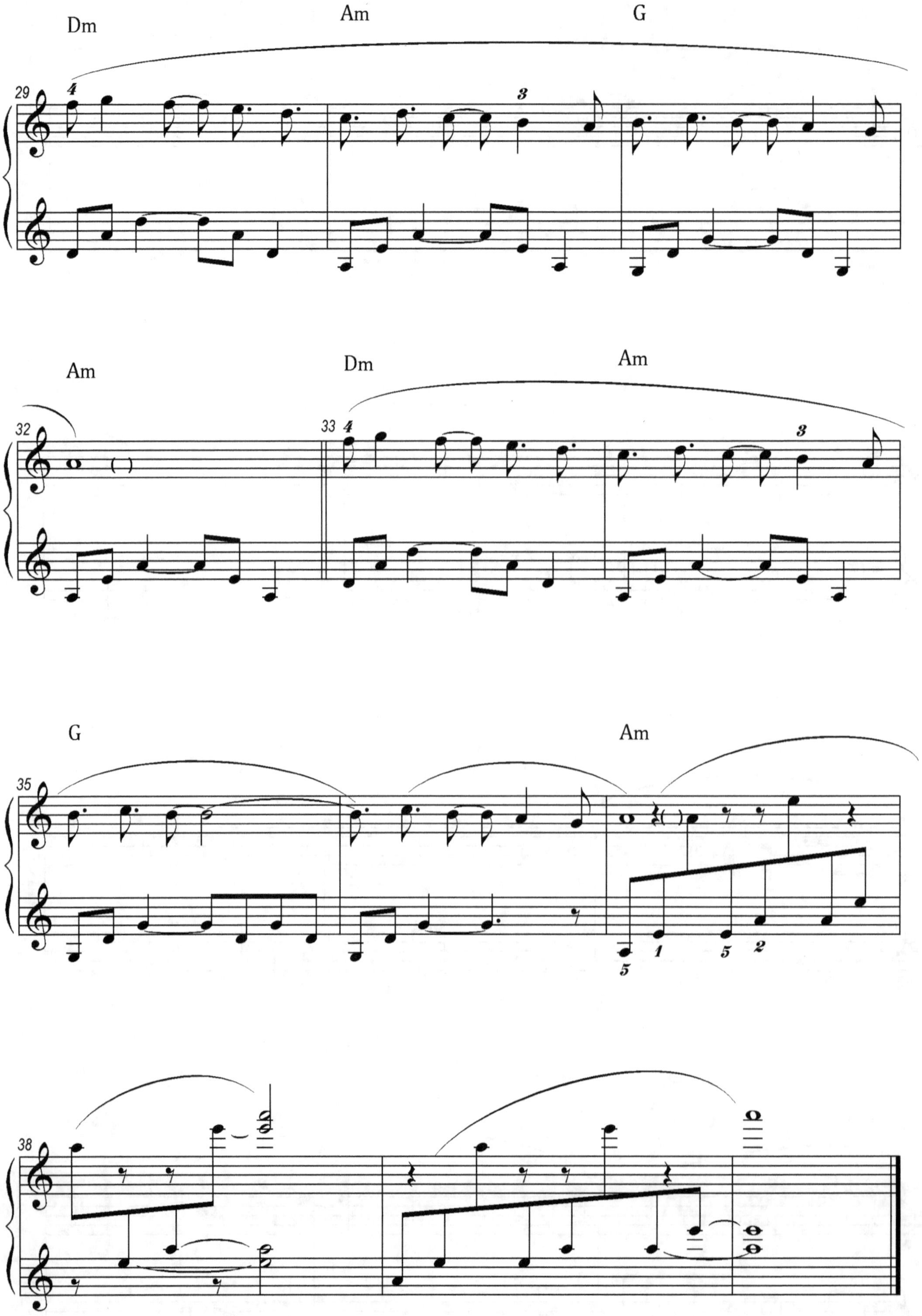

Dm
Am
G
29
Am
Dm
Am
32
33
G
Am
35
38

Three Fourths – E Minor Variations (TFEM)

Playing the same musical material in a different key – that is, in a different place on the keyboard – helps you appreciate its structure, and to become, eventually, a far more creative musician.

To demonstrate the versatility of the MEPS 'find and play' hand position and texture, this module presents the 'Three Fourths' material in E minor and in six-eight time, with several variations.

The video plays out the base material (the 'theme') to start with. Copy this 'skeleton music' as a preparation. The MS (written-out music, 'manuscript') for the first variation is on the next page. If necessary, pick up the MEPS hand positions from p.28.

TFEM perf	(Video)

Em	Bm	C	G	Am	Em	D	Em
falling a 4th		falling a 4th		falling a 4th		the tone-apart pair	
	one-note overlap		one-note overlap				

Expect to 'see' how this chord sequence is 'the same' as the previous module's.

Counting six-eight

Six-eight – six quavers in a bar – is technically known as a 'compound duple time' time signature. 'Duple' means having two main beats in a bar, and 'compound' indicates that each beat is split into three.

Here are the first bars of the module performance with the counts written in. You see the proper 'out loud' counting ("One-and-a two-and-a, one-and-a two-and-a) between the staves and the six 'quaver slots' marked up below.

MEPS: Three Fourths in E minor, six-eight

Further variations

A willingness to play around with the keyboard texture of material while leaving its harmony fundamentally unchanged lies at the heart of the creative keyboard work. Listen to this variation on the module performance and see if you can spot the difference.

TFEM_02

The difference is that the left hand thumb notes have all been tied. Here is the music.

In practice, you'd probably vary the tied/not tied mix. Here's one possibility.

The left hand thumbs are only tied where there is more than one note in

TFEM_03

the right hand.

Now that you've freed up that quaver slot 4, you could un-tie the treble note in that slot and play it again.

TFEM_04

Here's a variation which has turned the left hand part upside down.

TFEM_05 (Video)

Notice the two alternative solutions for the left hand fingering difficulty.

Most improvisations and compositions evolve like this – through a series of small developments of already-known material. Here's a whole version built on this pattern. Note the way the material gets back round to its repeat (bars 8 and 9), and how the extended ending uses the typical 'ladder' tricks in new ways (bars 19 and 20).

Another variation

If you have downloaded the supplementary audio/MIDI package, listen to:

TFEM_06

The three right hand joining-up notes that you use to walk between the thirds have been re-ordered. Here are the original and the new version of the first (Em–Bm) chord change played alternately so that you can compare them clearly.

TFEM_07

Here's the MS of that clip. Same, up, down 'melodic contour' arrows have been put in so you can see how the melody has been played around with.

Work out how the second and third strings of joining-up notes (C down to G and Am to Em) will sound, adapted in the same way.

The Em–D–Em section melody is now this:

Try to play the new version from these clues alone. If you need it, the MS is on the next page.

Finally, try to work out how the melodic variation referenced here re-orders the same three joining-up notes. There is no MS for this example, but you can watch the MIDI in MidiPiano if you need further help working it out

TFEM_08

MEPS: Three Fourths in E minor - Variation 1

MEPS: Three Fourths in E minor - Variation 2

Introducing Thirds (ITPC)

The third is the 'sweet' interval – no other interval walks around the keyboard so harmoniously. This applies equally to its inversion, the sixth (which we tackle next), and the tenth – the 'plus an octave' third. All three are, in effect, two-note chords.

Playing thirds (and sixths) accurately and fluidly in the right hand is considered a landmark step-up in traditional keyboard teaching, and any modern-styles keyboard player should be prepared to practice a lot to get them coming easily and sounding good.

Both intervals are particularly useful for filling out the essentially 'bare' harmony of the standard MEPS root-fifth-octave left hand. This module revisits the first two pairs of chords in this workbook and adds thirds in the right hand.

Thirds in C and D minor

Here is the skeleton music for the first of the module studies – before any syncopation or LH-pattern adjustment has been brought in.

ITPC_02

Now, pull the last two right hand thirds in each bar forward a half-beat.

ITPC_03

The count in the first bar counts off the left hand quavers. The count in bars 2 and 3 (and the next-to-last bar) shows where the syncopated right hand notes fall. Where there is no right hand note in that quaver slot, the count number is bracketed.

The finished study

Finally, knock out quavers 3, 4, 5 in the left hand. In the MS. the count i.e. "1 and 2 and 3 and" etc is put in so you can see where the hands play together, left, or right.

Thirds C & Dm | Video URL

Here is a two-bar repeating practice audio of just the main syncopated pattern (the first two bars, in C) with the knocked-out quavers.

ITPC_04

MEPS: Thirds in C and D minor

Thirds in E minor and D

Here is/are the ~~audio and MIDI~~ video URL reference file numbers for the video showing the build-up of syncopation for the E minor and D Thirds study.

| Thirds Em & D | (Video) |

Here's the base material.

ITPC_05

Next, bring forward all but the first right hand notes in every bar. In the music, just the E minor pattern is shown, with the counts and TLR analysis. The audio repeats the pattern in E minor and D.

ITPC_06

Now drop quavers 4 and 5 from the left hand pattern. Just the E minor pattern is shown and played.

ITPC_07

53

There is one more degree of syncopation possible – the first right hand note of the second bar is pulled forward over the bar-line. The first audio/MIDI plays the pattern in E minor only for practice; the second alternates E minor and D.

| ITPC_08 | ITPC_09 |

The finished study

The sections of the finished study are joined together with MEPS 'ladders' – ascending and descending patterns of just roots and fifths. These are great 'bar fillers' for your own improvisations and will improve your command of the whole keyboard.

Practice the ladders separately until they're smooth and reliable. The first one (bars 9 to 12) covers two octaves; the second one (bars 21 to 24) covers three octaves. Stems-up notes are right hand notes; stems-down notes are left hand. Watch the two sections of the video closely and copy those.

Here are the audio and MIDI reference file numbers for the finished second module study.

| ITPC Em and D | (Video) |

There is an archived video of the Thirds in E minor and D material. You might find it interesting to watch it and try copying or playing along.

| (Video) |

There is also and archived video of the C and D minor in Thirds study you might like to explore in the same spirit.

| (Video) |

MEPS: Thirds in E minor and D

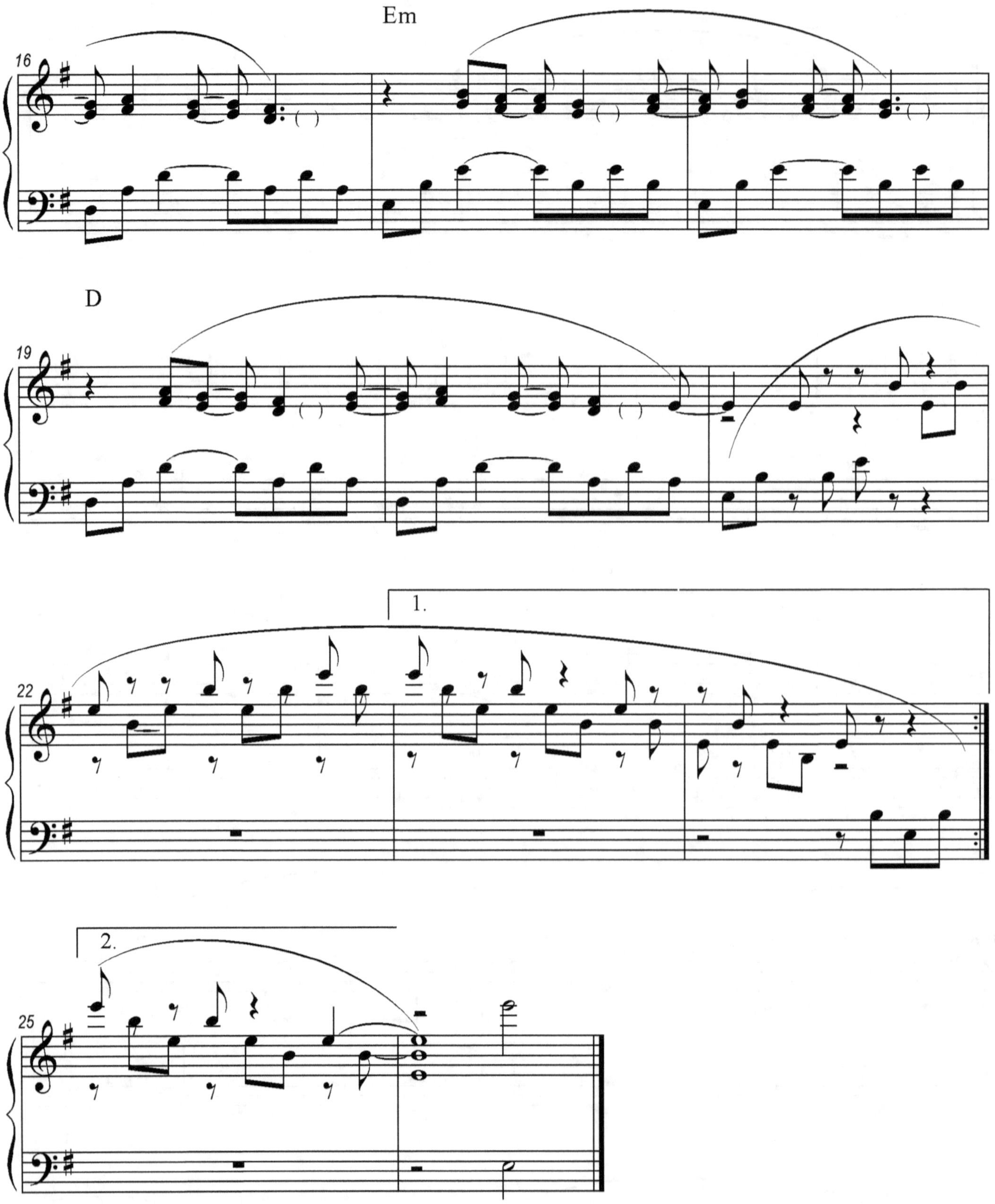
Em
16
D
19
1.
22
2.
25

Exercises for Thirds (EX3)

Piano technique is always a 'work in progress' It takes years to learn to play thirds well, so make a start no matter how you feel about your abilities. As with all technical benchmarks, little and often wins the day. Keep coming back; do a little (no matter how little) every day.

This collection of exercises is based on the requirements of the present volume and makes no claim to being definitive. Serious students of keyboard technique will have or acquire one or more of the many standard books of technical keyboard exercises.

There are five MIDI files/MMYT videos covering the whole set of exercises. The Midi files (If you have purchased the optional supplementary files) are numbered EX3_01–05. You can see the MidiPiano performances in the Technical Exercises playlist on MisterMusicarta YouTube (MMYT).

In order not to interrupt the flow of the volume, the MS of only the first set of exercises is placed here. The full set of exercises is at the back of the book.

The chief fault in playing thirds is that the two notes do not play together, but one after another. Listen and watch closely to check your own performance and adjust your technique accordingly.

Notice that legato ('joined-up') thirds are much harder to play than detached thirds. Settle for detached and work towards legato over time. Note also that if the top notes of a string of thirds are played legato, listeners will 'forgive' the lower notes not being perfectly joined up.

These exercises are presented in key of C major, and are therefore played on all-white piano keys. Once you have some facility, vary your practice by playing them in other major keys. You will immediately find the occurrence of black keys presents novel fingering challenges, but the essence of free keyboard playing is to get the notes out 'at any cost', so neat, predetermined, 'classical' fingering is not the priority.

Note that you can immediately transpose the MIDI files into other keys using the MidiPiano 'Key' facility. Exercises will then show on the keyboard in the new key.

Fingering

Fingering given for one section of the pattern will apply to the next section of the same length as well.

Sometimes, only the upper note fingering is given. Fingers 2 and 3 will take 1 (thumb) as the lower note, 4 will usually take 2 and 5 will take 3 – but be alive to other possibilities.

Watch out for alternative fingering (indicated). Try all types, and experiment with your own. One's own way of fingering thirds evolves and matures out of a number of equally available options.

Exercises for Thirds

Tanza

This little rhythmic study suggests a jazzy mediaeval dance. It uses a typical Aeolian mode* three-chord selection (A minor, G and F) plus the overlapping fourths construction of the 'Three Fourths' material, in this case falling from A minor. (The original falls from E minor. Playing the same chord sequence from different starting points – transposing it – gradually opens your eyes and ears to the inner workings of harmony and chord structures.)

Rhythmically, the dropped quavers in the six-eight meter together with the little syncopated 'kick' in the left hand offer new syncopation challenges. Study the counting and TLR sections below carefully.

Here are the chord sequence and file references.

'A' strain

Am	G	Am	G	Am	G	F :G	Am	F :G	Am

'A' strain extended ending – one bar

Am	G	Am	G	Am	G	F :G	Am	F :G	Am	Am

'B' strain

Am:Em	F :C	Dm:Am	G :Am	Am:Em	F :C	Dm:Am	G	G	Am	Am

(video performance has two additional bars of A minor)

Tanza perf	(Video)

Notes

Prepare by learning the skeleton music. (The skeleton music is shown at the bottom of the second page of MS, below.)

Tanza_02

Notice the odd line lengths – one ten-bar line and two eleven-bar lines. Music generally comes in multiples of four – eight bars in a line of popular music, for example – and different phrase lengths (and slight variations on them) make music more interesting to listen too.

Notice the difference between first- and second-time material, in both the A and B strains. In the repeat of the A strain, the left hand (in bars 12 and 16), catches the dotted quaver 'kick' from the right hand. It does the same thing in the second half of the B strain (bars 26 on). Small developments like these make repeated material acceptable to the listener and help you, the pianist, get more 'mileage' out of what you've learned.

---

* Modes are old-style musical keys – families of chords with a particular 'flavour' unlike the modern classical major and minor keys. Most of the music in the MEPS workbook is modal.

Notice how, in the first section, because the right hand uses the octave/root in the melody so much, the four notes of the MEPS note set are redistributed 'two and two', with the root and fifth (only) in the left hand, and the octave (root/'8') and third in the right.

left hand ⌐ ⌐ right hand

For the B section, the hands revert to the more usual three-plus-one distribution:

left hand ⌐ ⌐ right hand

⌐ left hand ⌐ right hand

⌐ left hand ⌐ right hand

Counting

Practice saying out loud the count of the typical *Tanza* rhythm. Often, in the case of tricky rhythms, "If you can say it, you can play it!"

"One two and three, two two and three, one two and three, two two and three"
(This is fast.)

A variation

As already mentioned, the creative keyboard player is always on the look-out for ways to get a bit more 'mileage' out of what he or she has already mastered.

Here's a simple variation on *Tanza*. The A strain is played hands crossed, left over right, with the left hand accompaniment quavers in slots 2 and 3, 5 and 6 only. The hands uncross for the B strain but the accompaniment is still delayed by a quaver.

Try to play the variation by ear. (There isn't any written-out music.) Play the MIDI file on MidiPiano for a more visual idea of the performance.

Tanza Variation

You could use the A strain part of this variation as a 'recap' (a recapitulation; a return of or restatement of some previously played material) for an extended ABA *Tanza* version.

Tanza

R A Chappell

Skeleton music

Afternoon

Afternoon piano solo was created, like all the pieces in this volume, using the four MEPS chord tones (root, fifth, octave and third) and signature rocking left hand.

Here are the chord sequence and the solo reference files.

1								
G	G/B:C	Em:Bm/D	C	C :G/B	D7/A:G	D7/F♯:A7/E	D

9							
G	G/B:C	Em:Bm/D	C	Em: D7/F♯	Cmaj7:Bm7	Am7:D7	G s–r

Ending

Em: D7/F♯	Cmaj7:Bm7	Cmaj7:D7	G sus-res

Afternoon perf	(Video)

Walking tenths

Afternoon makes particular use of the outer of the four MEPS chord tones – the lowest root and the highest tone, the third. Counted as a two-note interval, this pair of notes is called 'a tenth'.

Here is some 'skeleton music' which shows (mainly) just the tenths.

AFNN_02

You will learn this solo much more quickly if you play this music along to the audio or video performance file repeatedly, until it 'sinks in'.

Slash chords

If, however, all four chord tones moved in parallel with this outer pair, the result would not be very musical.

AFNN_03

Instead, the middle note doesn't change every time the outer pair of notes moves. The result is much more harmonious – and the basis of our solo.

AFNN_04

(As before, learning this music – from the MidiPiano MIDI file performance, for example – and playing along to the performance will greatly speed your learning of the piece, as well as your understanding of how chords and harmony work.)

This new type of movement gives rise to the chord symbols you see with a slash in them.

G/B   Bm/D   D7/A   D/F♯   A7/E

You read these as:

"G over B", "B minor over D", "D7 over A" etc., or

"G with a B in the bass" etc.

These chord symbols indicate that a note other than the root (name-note) of the chord is in the bass (the lowest sounding note).

Because of the slash in the symbol, these chords are known as 'slash chords'. A slash chord is a chord with a note other than the root in the bass.

Afternoon

R A Chappell

Em
D/F♯
Cmaj7
Bm7
Am7
D
13
1.
G sus res
2.
G sus res
Em
D/F♯
16
Cmaj7
Bm7
Cmaj7
D
G sus res

Other features

Sus-res

Sus-res (among the chord symbols) stands for suspension-resolution. A suspension is the pulling-up of a chord tone – usually the third – played noticeably on the beat. In *Afternoon*, it's note B, the third of the G chord, which gets pulled up to a C in bars 1 and 16 (plus repeats and ending) before being let back down. (The suspension is 'resolved'.)

Suspension-resolution is a great device for getting more out of the chords you know. Check the Suspensions tab on the Musicarta site navbar and the Suspensions playlists at MMYT and Musicarta Soundcloud to learn more.

Stemming and fingerings

As well as the sus-res marking, bars 1 and 2 show stemming – in bar 2 – which indicates that two notes are played by the left hand, and are therefore written in the bass clef, but are stemmed from the treble clef as well to indicate they are melody notes.

There are also left hand notes with two fingering numbers. This indicates that the note is played by the first of the two fingers but then 'handed over' silently to the second one for a legato (joined-up) sound. Watch the video performance for examples. This is an advanced, optional technique.

Ever True

Like most of the pieces in Musicarta Piano Solos Volume One, *Ever True* was created using the Musicarta Easy Piano Style keyboard improvisation techniques.

The piece only uses three chords (A minor and next-door G and F majors), and its form (structure) is ABA. The only difference in the B strain is that the left hand 'goes large'!

1, 17, 33 ('A strain')

Am	Am	G	G	Am	Am	G	G

9, 25 ('B strain')

F	F	G	G	F	F	G	G

41 (ending – ladders)

Am	Am	Am	Am

Ever True perf.	(Video)

In the A strain, the left hand follows the familiar MEPS technique of playing only some of the eight potential root-fifth-octave-fifth quavers in the bar.

All the quaver slots filled   Slots 3, 4, 5 'knocked out'   Slots 4 and 5 only knocked out

ET_02

The audio and MIDI files repeat each bar (as shown) and then play through again. Play along and practice counting your music out loud

The B strain left hand

In the B strain, the left hand plays the root-fifth-octave group an octave lower, plus the notes of a root position triad on top of that, and adds a joining ninth/second.

ET_03

(Notes continue after the MS.)

Ever True

R A Chappell

(optional jump to bar 33 for easy version)

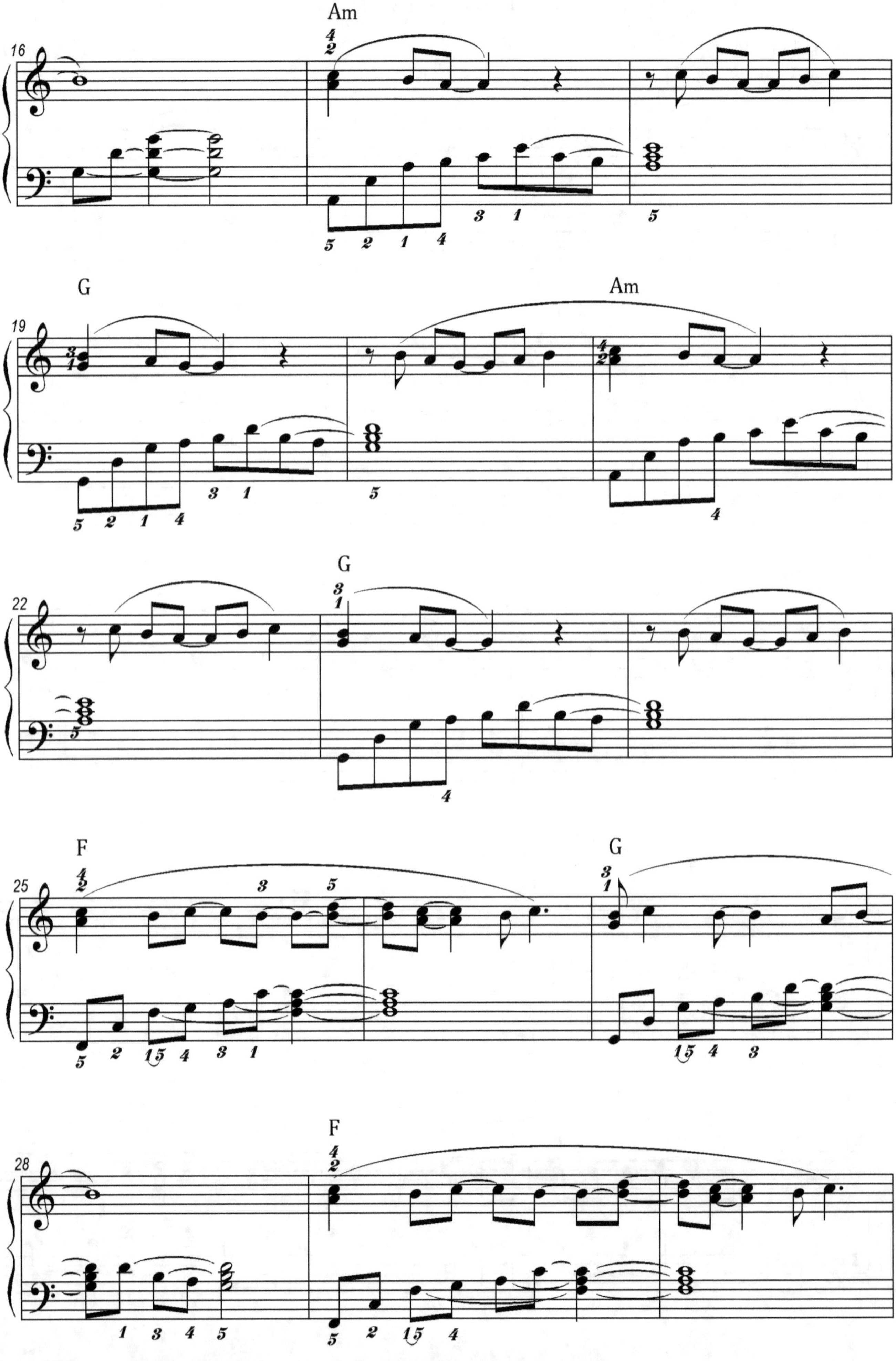

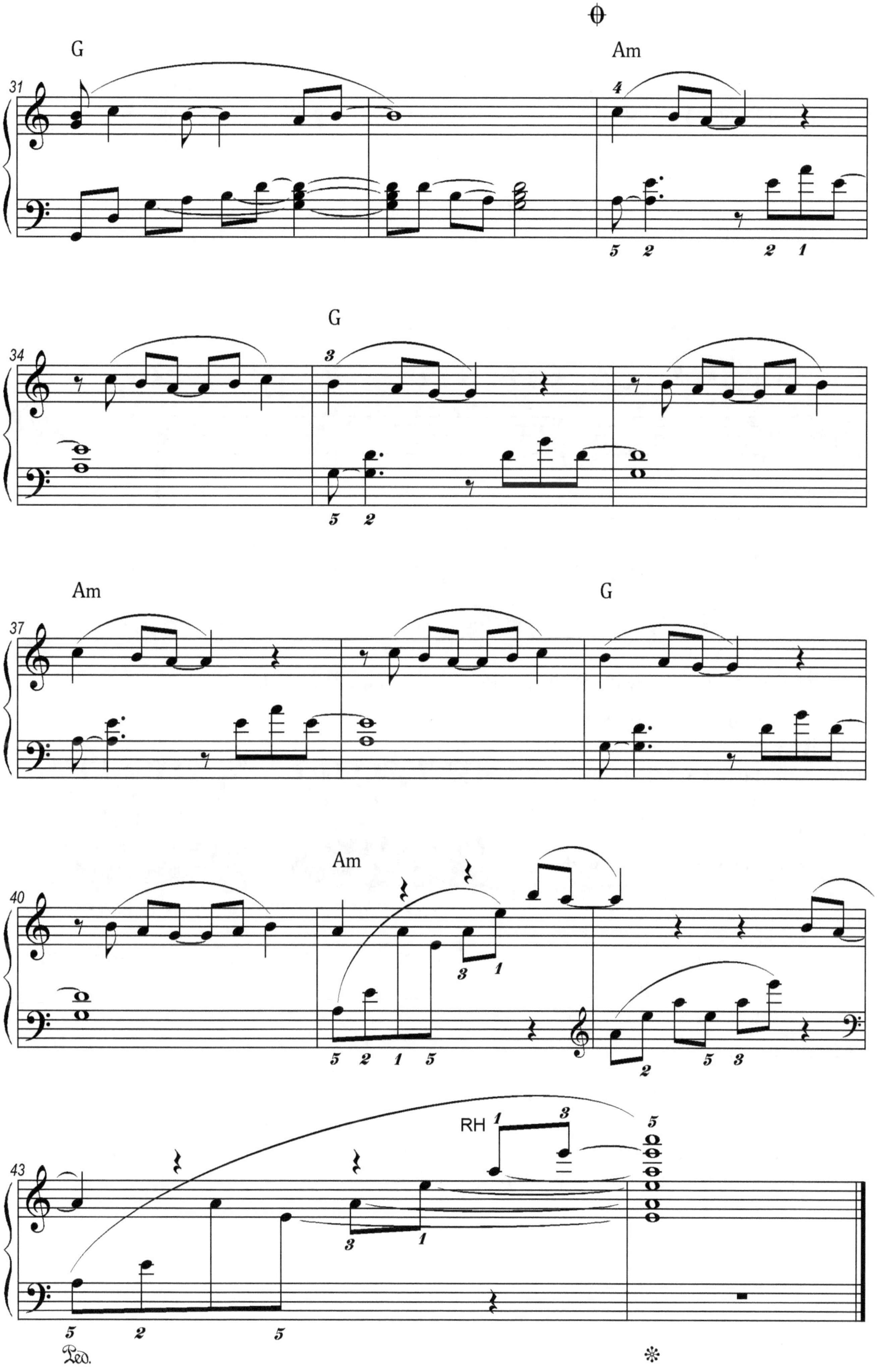
G
Am
G
Am
G
Am
RH
Ped.

These left hand notes are played a number of different ways. Practice them up and down to improve your accuracy and stamina, as shown in the second bar and the audio and MIDI reference files.

(Notice the alternative fingering given for notes B and C in the practice fragment.)

The advanced tying-over of notes in bars 17, 19 etc, and the passing of the octave from left hand fingers one to five without letting it up in bars 25, 27, 29 etc are optional.

Fingering the ladders

The piece ends with a series of root/fifth (R, 5) 'ladders'.

ET_04

These notes are all played by the left hand. Practice as in the audio clip.

The fifth is not midway between two roots – it's closer to the top note. So if you're playing two roots (root and octave) with a fifth in the middle, LH finger 2 is the best finger to use.

But if you're playing two fifths with a root between the, LH finger 3 is the better finger to use.

use LH finger 2

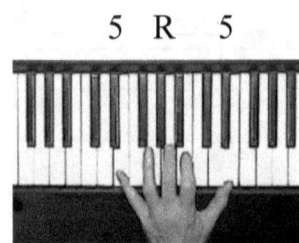

use LH finger 3

If you try to use finger 2 for the middle note in ladders all the time, you risk playing the wrong note in the fifth-root-fifth 'rung' of the ladder. If you keep hearing wrong left hand notes – check your fingering!

An optional easier version

It's frustrating to not be able to play a piece because of just one section! If the 'big left hand' section (bars 17 to 32) is stopping you playing this piece – or just until you've practised it enough – make a simpler version of this piece by jumping from the end of bar 16 to bar 33 (as indicated in the music) and playing from there to the end.

Fanfare

The four chords used in *Fanfare* are the four you're most likely to find in any piece of Western music. Expressed in the Roman numeral 'chords in any key' naming system, they are chords I, IV, V and vi. In *Fanfare* key of C major, they are C, F and G majors, plus A minor.

(An explanation of the Roman numeral system of naming chords can be found via the Chords tab on the Musicarta website navbar.)

Played C-Am-F-G (I-vi-IV-V), they are the chords of the keyboard novelty piece and of hundreds of rock'n'roll songs sketched in the first audio clip.

FANF_02

Taking the A minor chord as the starting point and re-ordered vi-IV-I-V, however, the chord set sounds much more imposing. Here are the chord sequence and reference files for *Fanfare*.

1, 9   *(repeats)*

Am	F :C	G :Am	F :C	G :Am	F :C	G	G

Extended ladder ending

C	C	C	C

Fanfare perf. | (Video)

Notes

Rehearse the hand positions used in Fanfare thoroughly before attempting the rhythmic texture. *Fanfare* covers a lot of the keyboard, so you may well need the orientation. Watch the MidiPiano performance through for a visual 'take'. The second half of the MMYT video shows just the skeleton music.

FANF_03

Notice how, on the two-handed ladder ending, the right hand leads going up the keyboard and the left hand leads coming down.

'Key chords' I, IV, V and vi are the chords covered in the Musicarta Key Chords Volume One digital home study download. You can explore this learning material via the Key Chords tab on the home site navbar and the MMYT Key Chords playlist.

Fanfare

R A Chappell

An Unsettling Notion

In this simple piece, the texture to start with divides the four basic MEPS chord tones (root, fifth, octave, third) two and two. The structure is A, B repeating. The difference between the A and B strains is only one chord. The repeat of A, B goes a little 'bigger' – the left hand includes the tenth (third) and the right hand some sixths.

The tonality (key) is A minor Dorian (four chords: A minor, G, D and C majors). The chord sequence, skeleton music and reference files for *An Unsettling Notion* are as follows.

1

| Am | G :D | Am :D | Am :D | Am | G :D | Am :D | Am :D |

9 (repeats)

| C | G :D | Am :D | Am :D | C | G :D | Am :D | Am :D |

33 (Extended ending)

| Am | G :D | Am :D | Am :D | Am | Am | Am | Am |

| ANUN perf | (Video) |

ANUN_02

Note the three different 'phrase end' bars: see bars 4, 12 and 16. The 'big' left hands in bars 9, 13, 17 etc. are all slightly different as well. In practice, you can prioritise the performance and let your own convenient finger/hand arrangement play out in these bars, and only look into the precise 'as written' version as and when it suits you.

Count off the three parts of the closing 'ladder'. They are seven notes ("1 & 2 & 3 & 4") twice, then nine notes – "1 & 2 & 3 & 4 & 1".

An Unsettling Notion

R A Chappell

Am G D Am D Am D
21
C G D Am D Am D
25
C G D Am D Am D
29
Am G D Am D Am D
33
molto rall.
37
slower
8va
rall. et dim
15ma
8va
Ped.

Introducing Sixths

(OFIS)

Like thirds, sixths are very harmonious and offer an easy way to harmonise melodies. (Sixths are thirds, inverted.) In this module, we're going to add sixths to the One Fourth and a Pair material to make 'One fourth in sixths' (OFIS).

Here's the module study final version audio reference. The video covers the whole build-up.

| OFIS final perf. | (Video) |

To prepare, revise this version of the 'One Fourth and a Pair' study on page 28.

OFIS_02

Now rehearse this skeleton music for the with-sixths version.

OFIS_03

Notice that the left hand has to play one octave lower to make way for the sixths.

Now add exactly the same syncopation as before (MS on next page). The ending only is new.

| OFIS_04 | (Video) |

One Fourth in Sixths - *first version*

R A Chappell

MM = 112

The next version of 'One Fourth and a Pair' is also good for the adding-a-sixth treatment. Revise the one-note version thoroughly first. (The MS is on page 33.)

OFIS_05

Here's a with-sixths version. Note some additional syncopation in the very first bar.

OFIS_06

Not all the right hand notes have sixths added – the sound gets too thick. This version already explores some different up/down 'contour' options (bars 5, 6, 7). Make little variations like these part of your 'final version'.

OFIS_01

One Fourth in Sixths - *final version*

Three Fourths in Sixths

(TFIS)

Once you can play the One Fourth in Sixths material, adding the sixth to the original 'three fourths' material to play 'Three Fourths in Sixths' is the obvious next step. Here are the module study file references. (The video covers the E minor variation as well.)

First, revise the Three Fourths and a Pair study from page 36.

Here is the skeleton music for the added-sixths version.

TFIS_02

The MS for the full performance is on the next page. The repeat (the second-time music) has more rhythmic smoothing in the right hand.

On the page after that is a version with a bigger left hand accompaniment.

TFIS perf
(Video)

TFAP perf
(Video)

TFIS perf

MEPS: Three Fourths in Sixths

R A Chappell

Three Fourths in Sixths, Version 2

The Version 2 left hand breaks out of the root-fifth-octave formula and plays some accompaniment figures which include the tenth (the third above the octave) as well.

The audio/MIDI reference for Version 2 on the previous page is: | TFIS V.2 perf |

The E minor six-eight version

On the next page, you will find the MS for a with-sixths version of the E minor, six-eight Three Fourths study.

Revise the one-note version on page 48 first.

| TFEM perf |
| (Video) |

Then make yourself a 'skeleton' practice with-sixths version. (You just add a second note in the right hand, a sixth below the melody note.)

Here's the MS and audio/MIDI reference. Note that you'll gain far more from working out how to do it at the keyboard than from just playing it from the music!

| TFIS_03 |

Here are the chord sequence and the audio/MIDI references for the full E minor sixths version. The keyboard texture is only a suggestion – try playing an E minor sixths variation of your own from just the chord sequence, if you at all can.

1, 9

Em	Bm	C	G	Am	Em	D	Em

17 - Extended ending

D	D	Em	Em

| TFIS Em Version perf | (Video)(second part) |

MEPS: *Three Fourths in Sixths, E minor, six-eight*

R A Chappell

Exercises for Sixths

Like thirds, the sixth is a 'sweet' interval, and, as you have seen in the last two modules, offers a great off-the-shelf way to harmonise a right hand melody. Modern-styles keyboard players should learn to play consecutive sixths fluidly and easily in their right hand, and the series of exercises presented here offers you a chance to start building this skill methodically.

Fingering sixths

There are two ways to finger consecutive sixths. The first is to 'set' your hand width, as if it were a calliper or protractors (see illustration), so the right hand thumb and little finger produce a sixth, and then walk your hand around the keyboard using a flapping wrist action.

This is '5-1 fingering', and is most practical when only or mostly white keys are being played. Good 'aim' is needed – your hand is essentially bouncing along.

The other way is 'legato fingering'. The top notes of the consecutive intervals are played as legato as possible using fingers RH3, 4 and 5. The thumb usually plays the lower note, but its 'hopping' character is masked by the smoothness of the upper note.

Most advanced of all is to finger both top and bottom notes legato using 5-2 and 4-1 fingering pairs. This can only be used for adjacent pairs of sixths.

In practice, an ad-hoc mixture of these approaches, often dictated by the distribution of any black keys in the run will usually evolve as the most convenient way of playing a particular sequence of intervals in a real piece of music. Only the legato fingering is given in the exercises, but '5-1' fingering should also be tried. All legato fingering should be taken as a suggestion only.

The movement in the exercises is always a strictly regular succession of steps or skips, which you will soon grasp. You should try to play the exercises without looking at the music as soon as you can – apart from a glance to establish what the pattern is.

The MIDI file of these exercises is included in the digital download. Using the MidiPiano 'Key' function you can transpose the exercises into any key. Playing whole exercises in black-key keys is very advanced keyboard work, but working out practical fingering for three- or four-interval sections of the exercises is certainly within the scope of the average MEPS student.

For your convenience a video of the exercises played in both C and D has been made. Here are the MIDI file and video references.

EX6_01	(Video)

Only one page of exercises is placed here – the full set is at the back of the workbook.

Exercises for Sixths

Sixths study - MEPS Diary 29-06-13   (SIST)

MEPS Diary entries are spontaneous keyboard compositions generated by combining the MEPS elements – the chord tones, the rocking root-fifth-octave left hand and a syncopated right hand – now with sixths.

MEPS Diary 29-06-13 (*A Dilemma*) is a study in sixths with a particular emphasis on syncopation patterns. Harmonically, MEPS 29-06 is in A Aeolian mode. (Read up on modes via the Modes tab on the Musicarta website.) Structurally, the study is in three-part ABA form. (You may find this 'aerial view' of a piece will help you learn more quickly and give you a more secure performance.)

Here are the chord chart and the module study file references.

1

Am	Am	F :G	Am	Am	Am	F :G	Am

9

F :G	C :F	Dm7:G	C		F :G	Am :F	Dm7:G	

16

Am	Am	F :G	Am	Am	Am	F :G	Am

MEPS 29-06 perf	(Video)

Skeleton music

With heavily syncopated music, make a habit of working out the underlying 'straight' version first. Not only will it help you learn the piece, but you can play it over and over and let the syncopated feel creep in naturally. Here is a skeleton-music MS sketch of MEPS 29-06-13. The music shows the hand positions – there are many shared notes.

SIST_02

Syncopation drills

MEPS 29-06-13 has been chosen for a thorough set of syncopation drills (see after MS).

The right-hand sixths at the start of the melodic phrases in the study never come on the first beat of the bar, but always just after – and in three distinct ways. Distinguishing between these – and learning to play them – will be an important step-up in your contemporary keyboard styling.

The first eight bars of music show all three varieties. In this annotated version, the left hand music has been lowered an octave to make room for the count and TLR mark-up.

Type 1   Type 1

(1)   2 & (3) & (4) &   (1) & (2) & (3) & (4)   (1)   2 & (3) & (4) &   (1)
L L T R   T L T   L T L R   T L L   L L T R L T L R   L

Type 2   Type 3

(1) & (2) & (3) & (4) &   (1) & (2) & (3) & (4)   (1&)a(2)& (3) & (4) &   (1)   (4)$ a
L T L R   T L T   L T L R   T L L   L L R L R L T L R   L

SIST_03

Put this excerpt audio/MIDI file on repeat in your media player and watch-and-listen until you can identify the three varieties of syncopation. In order of occurrence, they are:

- Type 1: On count "2" (= quaver slot 3) in bars 1 and 3;
- Type 2: On count "1 and" (= quaver slot 2) in bars 5, 17, 20, 24 and 26; and
- Type 3: On count "1 and a" (between the two above types, in quaver slot 1½) in bars 7 and 22.

In the end, the particular types of syncopation used in a performance is a matter of 'feel' and probably unconscious. In this piece, the first two types are definitely interchangeable, and the third type (the most difficult) could be considered optional. Total fidelity to the written music – and conscious choice while playing freely – can be a longer-term goal, but you will want to practice the three types conscientiously to really tighten up the timing. These types of syncopation crop up in all modern styles of keyboard playing, so your efforts will not be wasted.

To help you practice effectively the syncopation drills that   SIST_04 | (Video)

A Dilemma
(MEPS Diary 29-06-13)

R A Chappell

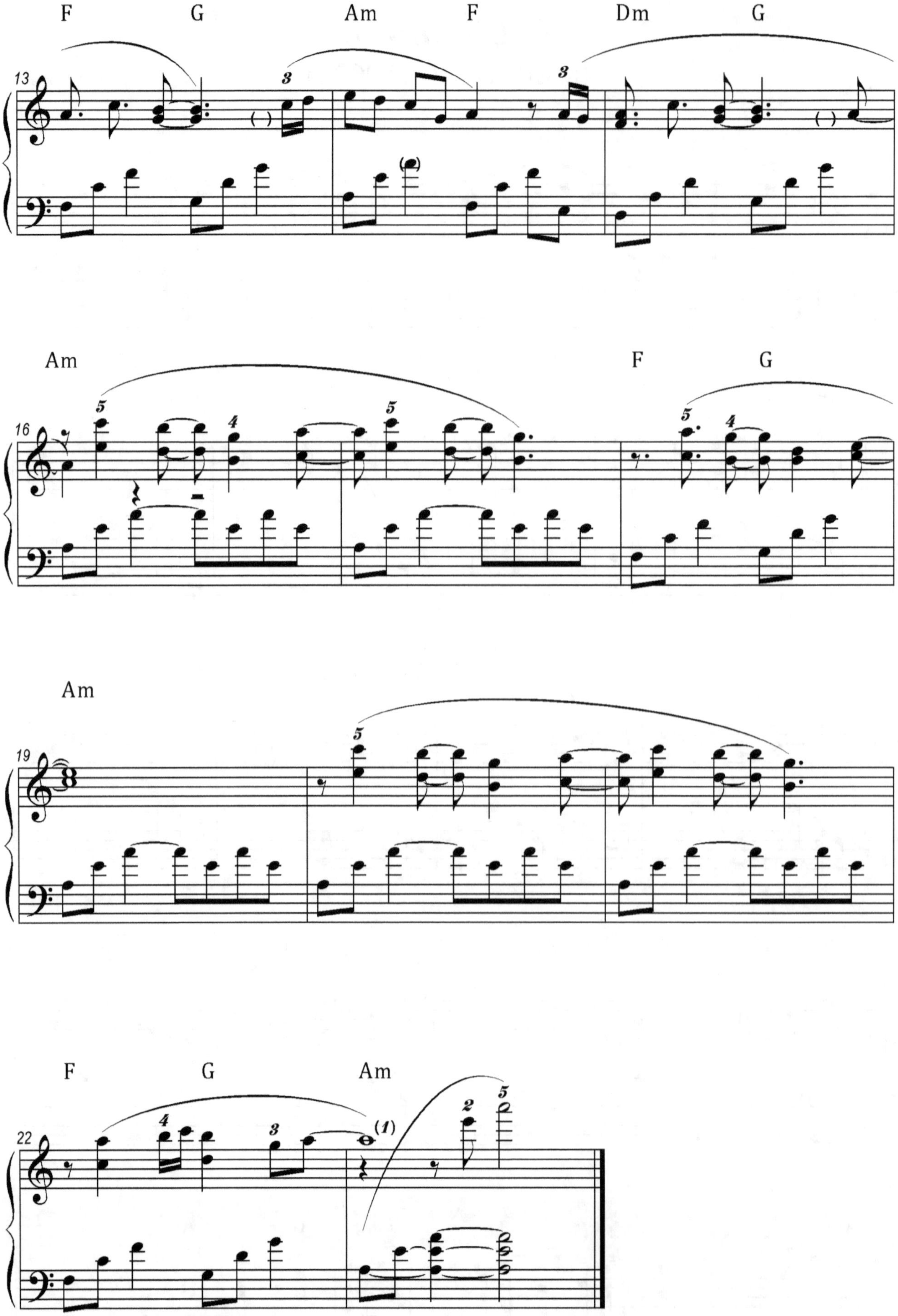
F G Am F Dm G
13
Am F G
16
Am
19
F G Am
22

MEPS Diary 29-06-13 - Syncopation Drills

The sixths played 'straight'

...over all-quavers left hand   ...over dropped-quavers left hand

Type 1 syncopation

Type 2 syncopation

Type 3 syncopation

Type 1 conttinuous   Type 2 continuous

SIST_04 (Video)

Working through these segments one at a time until you're comfortable playing them will greatly improve your contemporary keyboard styling.

- Bars 1 to 16: All three types are drilled, firstly over the standard full eight-quaver MEPS ostinato left hand, then over the typical 29-06-13 dropped-quavers pattern.

- Bars 17 to 22: The three types are repeated continuously over the 29-06-13 dropped quavers pattern.

- Bar 23 on: Real-time combinations of types are drilled, with an ending.

'Smoothed' rhythm

If you have right hand notes on count 1 in a Type 3 bar as well, you have the 'smoothed' rhythm referred to throughout this MEPS volume. You play this rhythm in bars 9 and 11 (and 13 and 15). Here are bars 9 to 12, marked up for counts and TLR analysis. Note that the left hand music is again written an octave lower to make room.

SIST_05

The audio/MIDI files are for bars 9 to 15 as a repeating section (for practice purposes).

If necessary, until you can reproduce the 'smoothed' rhythm, play bars 9, 11, 13 and 15 in either Type 1 or Type 2 rhythm. Alternating types works well.

SIST_06

The audio/MIDI files are for bars 9 to 15 as a repeating section (for practice purposes).

Note the re-harmonisation of material in the middle section (bars 9 to 15 – MS above). The F – G material in bar 9 is re-harmonised Dm7 – G in bar 11, and the C – F material in bar 10 is re-harmonised Am – F in bar 14. This is achieved in both cases by leaving the right hand (treble) material where it is and dropping the root a third – a composition technique known as mediant substitution. Try it yourself on any MEPS material!

95

Riff in Sixths - MEPS Diary 12-11-13   (SIRI)

Keyboard players are often required to play live accompaniments for a whole song. Small variations in what is essentially the same riff played over and over keep the music interesting for everyone.

These variations should be patterned in some way. The listener notices this, often subconsciously, and is carried along by expectation of the pattern unfolding. The pattern helps the player too, by providing an 'aerial view' of where you are in the piece, how far there is to go and so on.

MEPS Diary 12-11-13 is an opportunity not only to learn a 'groove' you can slip into (and a possible accompaniment to some soloing) but also an invitation to compose by combining and ordering subtle variations on a riff.

Here are the performance reference files.

MEPS 12-11-13 perf | (Video)

Finding the notes

MEPS 12-11-13 plays a set of three rising and falling sixths in C major, B flat major, A minor and G major.

SIRI_02

In fact, you see immediately that the B flat material doesn't stay true to type. The E natural (note) is not used, so the F does double shift.

The right hand music above is written crotchets-and-quavers only, but in practice the right hand in MEPS 12-11-13 is 'smoothed' throughout. Here are the sixths (plus the B flat variant) played the other way up and written and played in the smoothed rhythm.

SIRI_03

The first performance

Move straight on to a performance according to the following chord chart. The sixths are rising-then-falling and the left hand drops quavers 4 and 5 (counts "and 3"). If you can't play the smoothed rhythm yet, fit the five right-hand pairs of notes into the bar any way you can – on a 'just keep going' basis.

| Am | G | Am | G | C | Bb | Am | G |

SIRI_03

You might prefer to start off with an all-the-quavers version. Below is a practice segment, with the smoothed rhythm, which repeats. With the all-quavers version, you can see exactly where the right-hand in-between notes fall.

SIRI_04

97

Changing the shape

Our overall sound can be improved dramatically by cutting short the right hand in every other bar.

SIRI_05

You now have up-and-down followed by up-only patterns. Sketched out, that performance looks like this:

Am	G	Am	G	C	B♭	Am	G
⋀	⁄	⋀	⁄	⋀	⁄	⋀	⁄

Now play this version, from just the sketch music.

Am	G	Am	G	C	B♭	Am	G
⋁	＼	⋁	＼	⋁	＼	⋁	＼

SIRI_06

Now try up-and-downs with the even-numbered bars swapping type.

Am	G	Am	G	C	B♭	Am	G
⋀	⁄	⋀	＼	⋀	⁄	⋀	＼

SIRI_07

Combine the first and second halves of the previous two versions.

Am	G	Am	G	C	Bb	Am	G
⌄	＼	⌄	＼	⌃	／	⌃	＼

SIRI_08

Note that this work, with its attention to detail, is excellent training for playing by ear.

The performance matrix

You should be expecting to reach a point where you can hear the music represented by the up/down shorthand sketches above, and also possibly hear a version in your head and jot it down using this up/down shorthand.

The Musicarta performance of this riff (with some additional fancy finger-work and add-ins) follows the following overall pattern.

1 – First chorus

Am	G	Am	G	C	Bb	Am	G
⌃	／	⌃	／	⌃	／	⌃	＼

9 – Second chorus

⌃	＼	⌃	＼	⌃	＼	⌃	＼

17 (etc.)

⌄	＼	⌄	＼	⌄	＼	⌄	＼

25

⌃	／	⌃	／	⌃	／	⌃	＼

33

⌃	＼	⌃	＼	⌃	＼	⌃	＼

41

⌄	＼	⌄	＼	⌄	＼	⌄	＼

49 – Extended ending – repeat and fade

Am	G	Am	G	Am	G	Am	G
⌃	／	⌃	＼	⌃	／	⌃	＼

MEPS 12-11-13 perf | (Video)

The performance fancy

The best way to learn the right hand ornamenting tricks in the Musicarta performance is to listen closely to a repeating segment (at practice speed), and study the MIDI in MidiPiano. (The correctly written out music is given below, for reference.)

Here's what one two-bar pattern looks like in the MidiPiano Piano Roll pane.

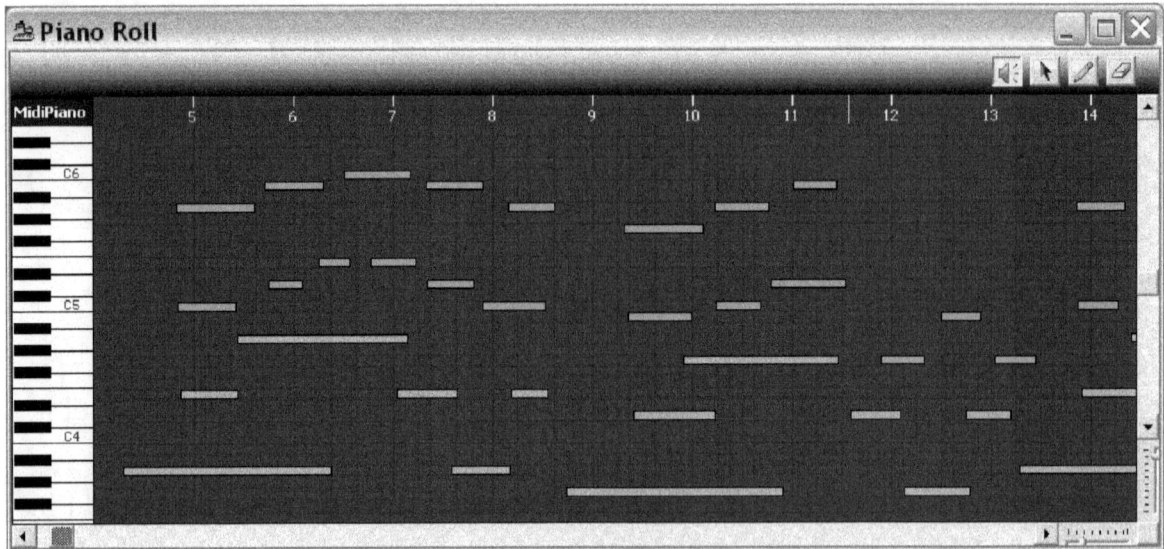

SIRI_09

Features are:

- Some of the right hand sixths are 'staggered' – the bottom note plays first;
- One of the sixths is staggered and 'shaken' bottom-top-bottom too; and
- There's an off-the-beat three-note right-hand counter-melody in the bass to fit in.

Here is the two-bar pattern shown above, so you can see how the notes line up.

Full MS for the Musicarta performance is not given. Copy as best you can, and practice whatever approximation you can get keep going relentlessly until it's uniquely your own.

Tanza (revisited, with sixths)

Sixths, like thirds, offer a simple but effective way of harmonising melodies. In this module, we revisit the Tanza piano solo and give it 'the sixths treatment'. The essential musical material remains the same, but the A and B strains are played a second time with the right hand an octave higher and harmonised with sixths.

Here are the chord sequence and file references.

'A' strain

Am	G	Am	G	Am	G	F :G	Am	F :G	Am

(The A strain plays through only once in the with-sixths section.)

'B' strain

Am:Em	F :C	Dm:Am	G :Am	Am:Em	F :C	Dm:Am	G	G	Am	Am

(The B strain again has a two-bar extended ending.)

Tanza Sixths perf   (Video)

The audio/MIDI/video files above cover only the new with-sixths material. The full *Tanza Revisited* performance is referenced below.

Skeleton music

You will benefit greatly from sketching out the component chords and the movement over the keyboard using this 'skeleton music'.

T6_02

The with-sixths material starts at bar 33, halfway down the second page of the full MS.

Playing sixths with all the melody notes would produce a very 'thick' sound, so only the on-the-beat notes come with the interval. It's still quite advanced keyboard technique, though. Graduate from the skeleton music to exercises like the following to work up the necessary combination of strength, flexibility and accuracy.

T6_03

T6_04

You should make a habit of creating little 'drills' like this for particular keyboard challenges. You will also want to use the Exercises for Sixths on page 88 and at the back of the book to build up your modern keyboard styles 'bag of tricks'.

In the B section, notice that the recommended fingering skips to RH4 for the top note of the second sixth in a pair. You might be able to stretch to RH2 (plus the thumb) for that final sixth. Try both, and feel free to develop your own fingering for this falling-fourths section. Watch your right hand thumb closely – it's the digit mostly likely to misplace.

The full performance of the Tanza is referenced here. The video shows a MidiPiano performance only.

Tanza Revisited full perf	(Video)

Tanza

R A Chappell

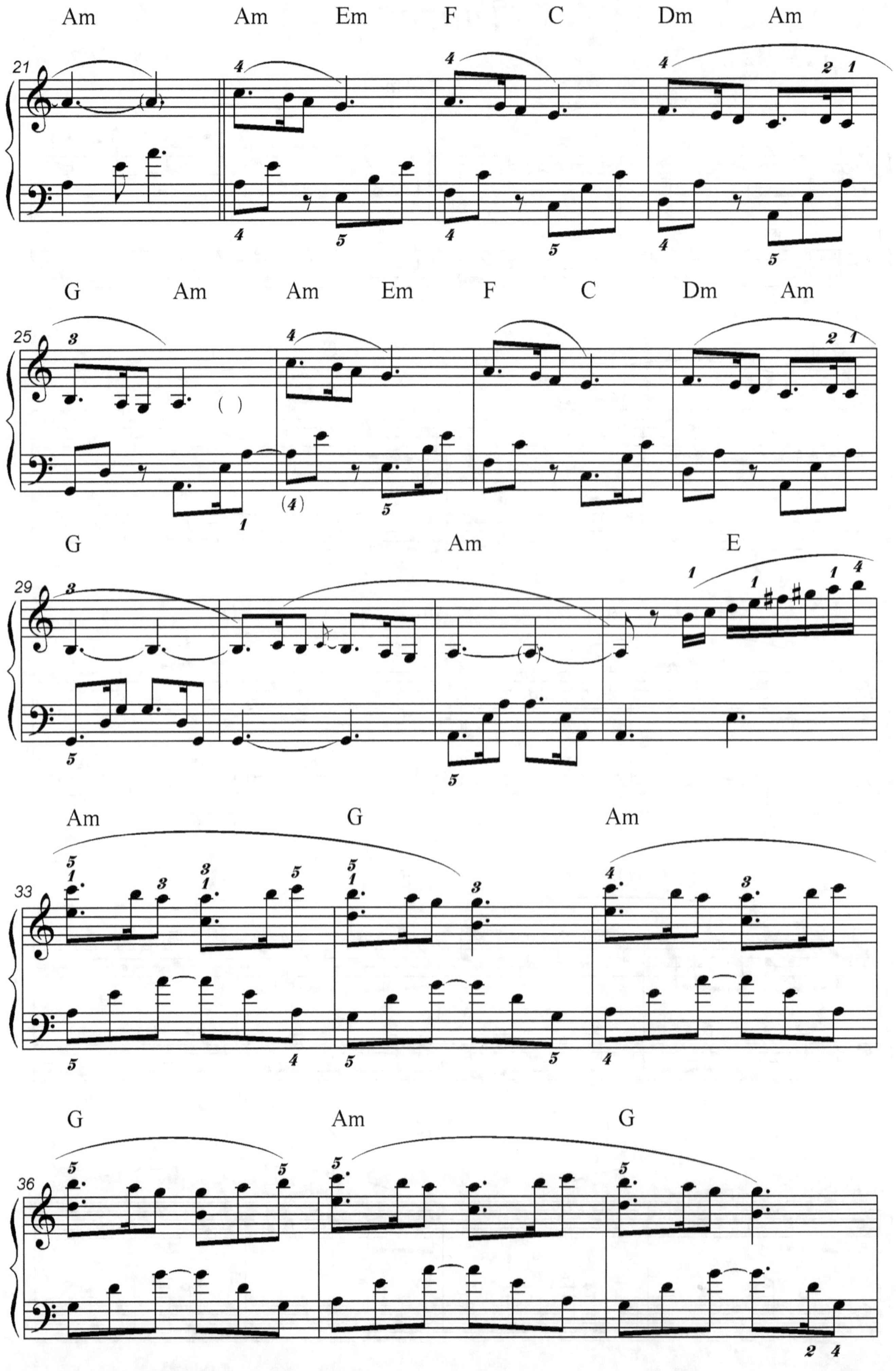
Am Am Em F C Dm Am
G Am Am Em F C Dm Am
G Am E
Am G Am
G Am G

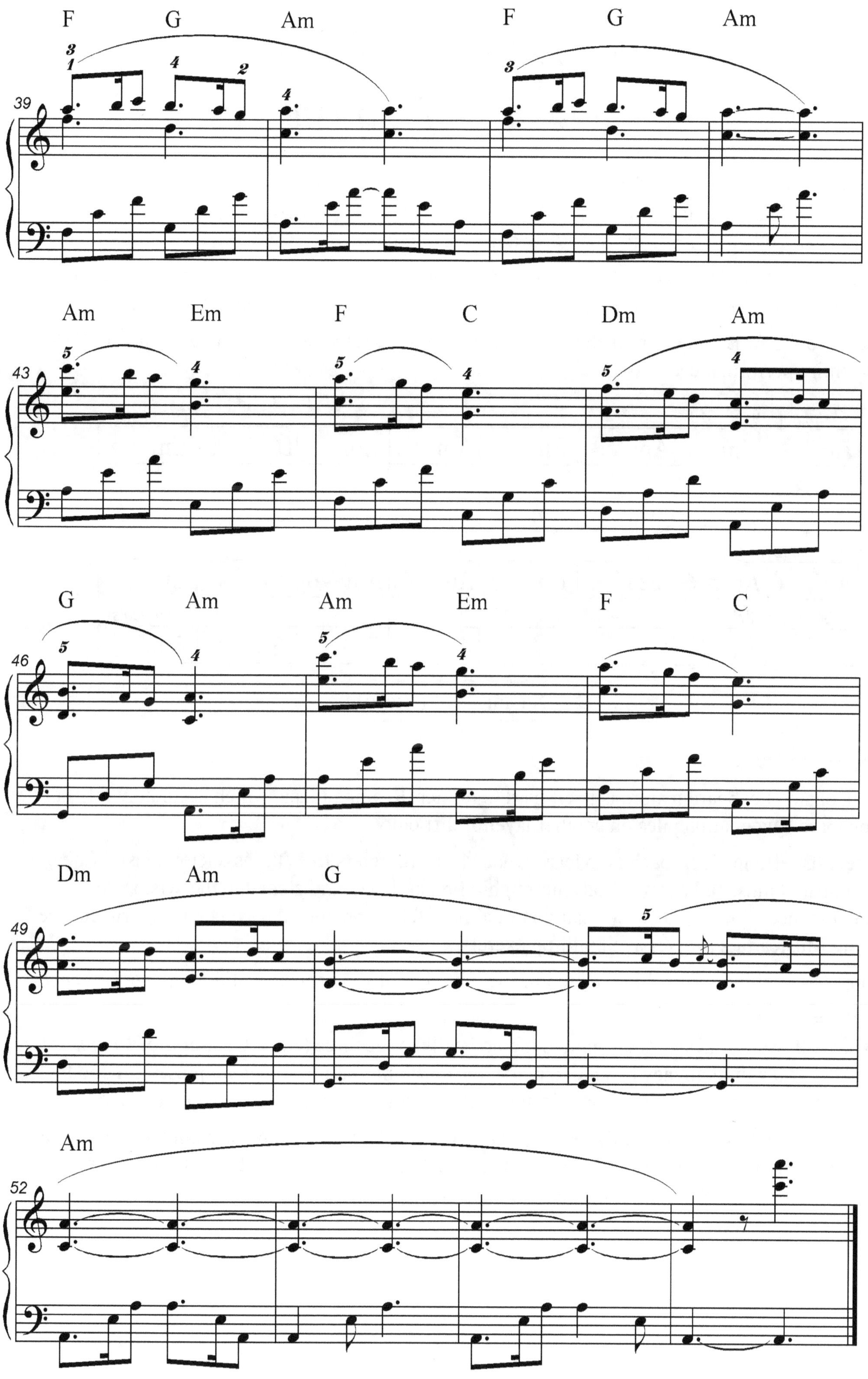
F G Am F G Am
39
Am Em F C Dm Am
43
G Am Am Em F C
46
Dm Am G
49
Am
52

Naomi – Fantasie

Naomi is the centrepiece of this Musicarta Easy Piano Style volume, and is a keyboard improvisation (a 'fantasie' or fantasia) incorporating the MEPS study, 'One Fourth in Sixths' (OFIS) and other typical MEPS textures and constructions.

The first part of Naomi (the 'A strain') is the simple, first version of One Fourth in Sixths (page 82). The two additional sections ('B' and 'C') are arranged in a symmetrical ABCBA structure.

Here are the A, B and C strain chord sequences, with the reference files and the video URL for the entire performance.

'A' strain (1, 9, 53, 61)   (repeats)

Am	Em	Am	Em	Am	Em	D	Em

(extended ending – 17, 69)

D	D	Em	Em

'B' strain (21, 45)

Am: ~6	Am:~6	Em	Em	Am: ~6	Am:~6	Em	Em

'C' strain (29, 37)   (repeats)

Am	Am	G	G	D	D	Em	Em

Naomi perf	(Video)

Skeleton music

Syncopated keyboard texture is itself hard to master. Reading music which accurately reflects keyboard syncopation piles on another layer of difficulty.

The most efficient approach is to learn what Musicarta refers to as the 'skeleton music' (the un-syncopated musical base material) thoroughly first and, having listened to the syncopated performance so that you know what you're aiming for, to practice the syncopated performance using Musicarta's progressive build-up exercises.

The *Naomi* video shows this skeleton music with the fully syncopated MidiPiano performance playing out below.

What follows is this approach applied methodically to the three (A, B, C) strains of *Naomi*. Ideally, you would already be able to play One Fourth in Sixths, but *Naomi* presents a good opportunity to revise the build-up of syncopation, and is written up as a standalone module.

The full written-out syncopated MS is given at the end of this module – accomplished classical readers can jump straight to it if desired. The skeleton music follows after that, to support a more intuitive approach and as an aid-to-memory.

The A strain

NAO_02

The section has an extended ending.

NA0_03

Rehearse the movement of the 'ladder' ending a few times – it's good if, however good you performance, you finish with a professional-sounding ending. Here is the ladder ending, written out. The same treble B and E notes are played first by the right hand, then by the left.

NAO_04

You might find it helpful to play the right hand 'straight' over an all-the-quavers left hand before syncopating it and dropping quavers out of the accompaniment.

NAO_05

In the fully syncopated version of the A strain only the very first A minor sixth is on the beat. The rest of the sixths are anticipated, and come with the left hand finger 2 – the 'and' (&) finger.

Here's a practice version with all the left hand quavers still in.

NAO_06

This screen-shot from MidiPiano shows all the sixths except the first one lining up with the middle of the left hand bottom-middle-top notes – left hand finger 2. This is a useful tip for placing them correctly, even if it feels strange at first.

The dropped-quavers versions

Here's a 'half-way house' exercise for the dropped-quavers version where the left hand plays only five quavers on counts 1 & 2 & 3.

NAO_07

Note the 'together, left, right' analysis (T, L, R) between the staves. A little time spent patiently working out 'what comes with what' can save a lot of time and frustration.

Any of these versions might be as far as you're able to get for now ('half-way house' performances) – or they could be variations-for-variety in your final performance. Either way, if you have the ladder ending perfected, you always have something you can play.

Now here is the actual performance A strain.

NAO_08

The left hand quavers come on counts 1 & 2... & 4. Use the TLR analysis and the counts between the staves to learn more efficiently

Here's an exercise for the D – E minor change in the extended ending of this section. The left hand plays on 1 & 2 ... & 4 &. (This is the actual final left hand.) You should make a habit of devising short, repeating practice segments like this for the various syncopation challenges in your playing.

NAO_09

Now all you need to do is add your practiced ladder ending. Here are the audio and MIDI files for the whole Naomi first section.

NAO_10

The B strain

Learning Musicarta material like *Naomi* methodically as suggested here is not only an efficient way of learning any piece. It also teaches you 'music', showing you, in effect, how to become a creative keyboard player.

Here is the skeleton music for the B strain.

NAO_11

When you break up the left hand into quavers for the Am/Am6 bars, anticipate the new chord – move the middle finger in advance. Here's a useful exercise.

NAO_12
(left)

NAO_13
(below)

Looking at the actual performance now:

Both the Am/Am6 and this E minor left hand movements warrant some dedicated practice. Reversing through movements is a good way of making sure the hand really knows where the notes are. Use the following exercises.

NAO_14

The audio/MIDI files run through all three exercises as written (with repeats) with a short pause between them.

Treat the right hand Am/Am6 figure similarly.

NAO_15

The C strain

The C strain looks like quite a lot of music, but almost half of it is repeated material.

NAO_16

After your skeleton music run-through, follow the procedure for the A strain and play the skeleton music over an all-the-quavers left hand.

NAO_17

Then play the syncopated right hand part over the all-quaver left hand.

NAO_18

Bars 5 and 6 of this music are slightly different in the repeat. Check bars 41 to 42 in the full MS for details. (Notice also that this version of the C strain shows none of the final-performance rhythmic 'smoothing'. See the section below for detailed analysis.)

Now you're ready for the dropped-quavers version – again, here presented without the smoothed rhythm.

NAO_19

The TLR analysis and counts are written in between the staves, if you need to break it down that far. Notice that the fifth bar of the music above breaks the pattern – you can play the left hand like bar 6 (on quavers 1 & 2 … & 4 &) if you wish.

The best way to learn to practice the full two-handed pattern is to get the left hand going then try to perfect just one two-handed two-bar pattern at a time.

NAO_20

Notice that the first right-hand bar of this exercise is again simplified slightly – the 'wobbled' sixth, as in the actual performance, comes only on the repeat. Always feel free to strip out any minor variations in the Musicarta material for the sake of getting a satisfactory performance going.

The 'smoothed' rhythm

In the smoothed rhythm, some of the crotchet-plus-quaver pairs are 'smoothed' into two equal dotted quavers.

Here is an exercise for the smoothed rhythm. Watch the MIDI performance on MidiPiano for a picture of 'what goes with what'. (The second note of the smoothed right hand pair comes between two left hand quavers.)

NAO_21

You can put as much or as little of the rhythmic smoothing into your performance as you wish or are able. The rhythmic smoothing in the Musicarta MEPS material is a prelude to freer independent right hand rhythm (*rubato*), which naturally takes time to develop.

Your complete performance

You have now rehearsed all the parts of *Naomi*.

Now, work at your complete performance. Identify weak areas (where you make mistakes or stop altogether) and revise the practice recommendations for those parts.

The MS for the entire piece follows, with the skeleton music after it. At any stage, you can experiment with playing *Naomi* from the skeleton music – you might find it easier than looking at the complicated, full written-out MS.

The skeleton music can also help you play the piece from memory. In addition, you might come up with a simpler 'work-around' version that you can play right through from start to finish, or a variation you like – always an acceptable outcome.

Naomi - Fantasie

R A Chappell

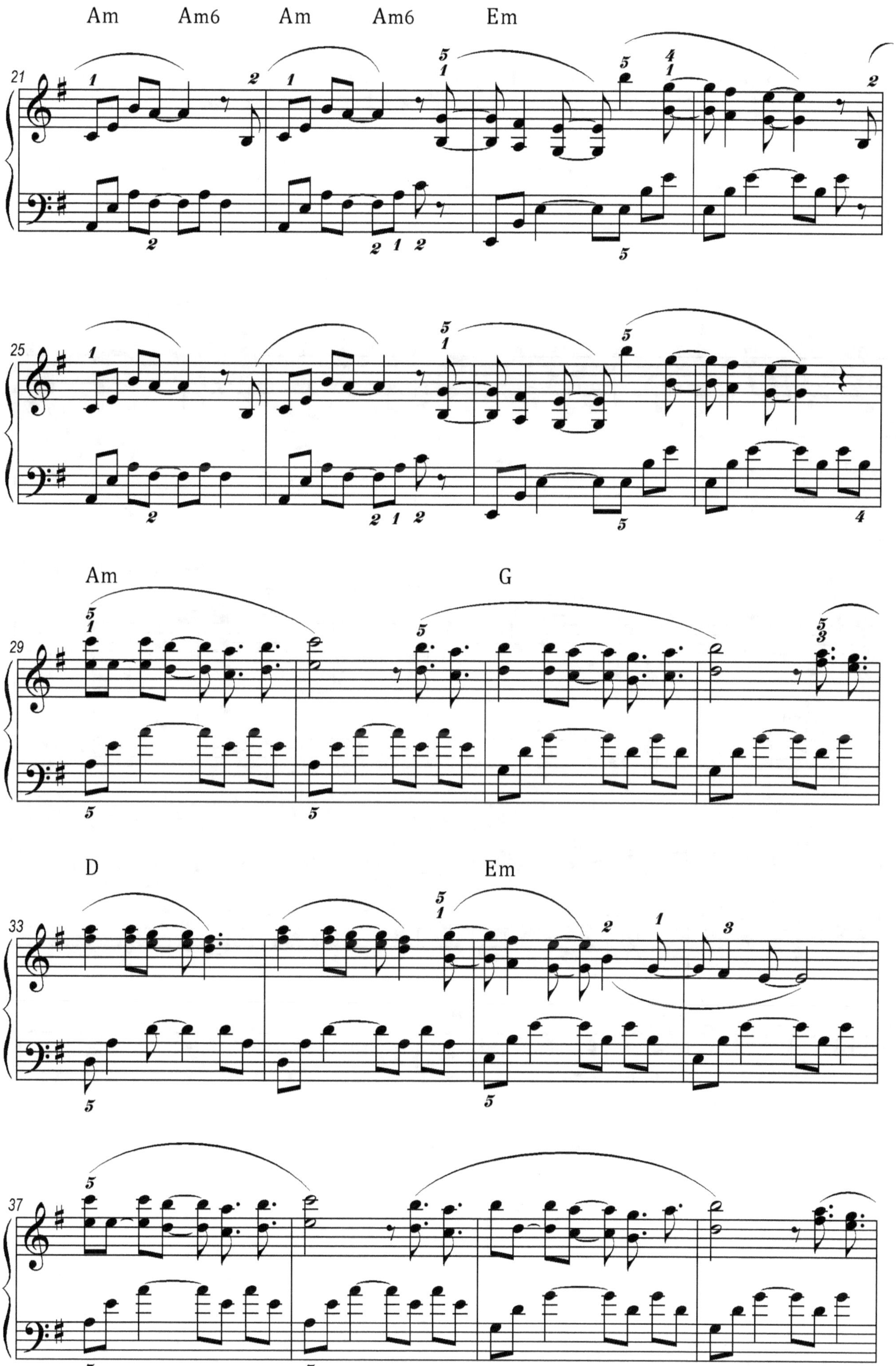
Am
Am6
Am
Am6
Em
Am
G
D
Em

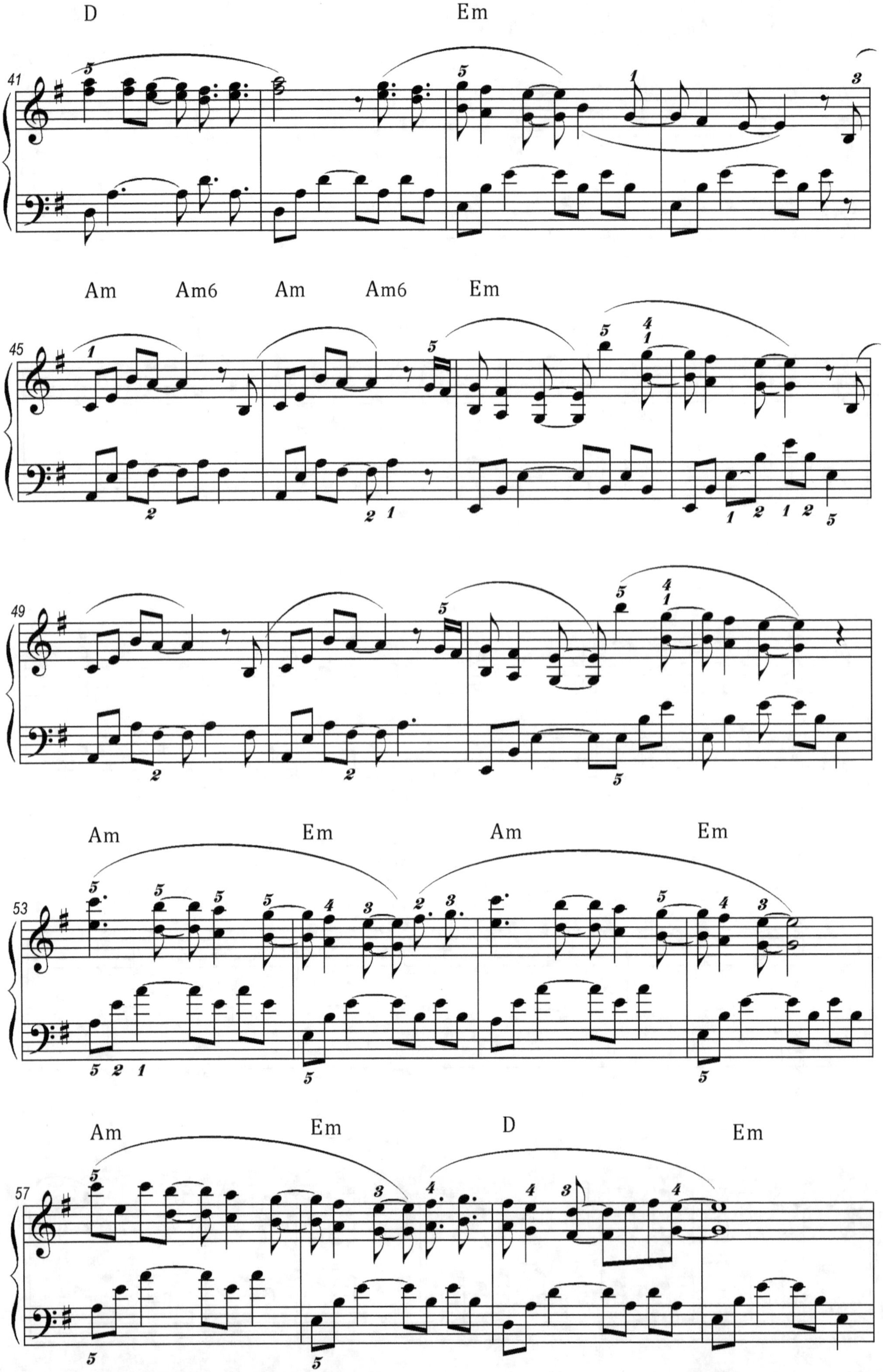
D Em
41
Am Am6 Am Am6 Em
45
49
Am Em Am Em
53
Am Em D Em
57

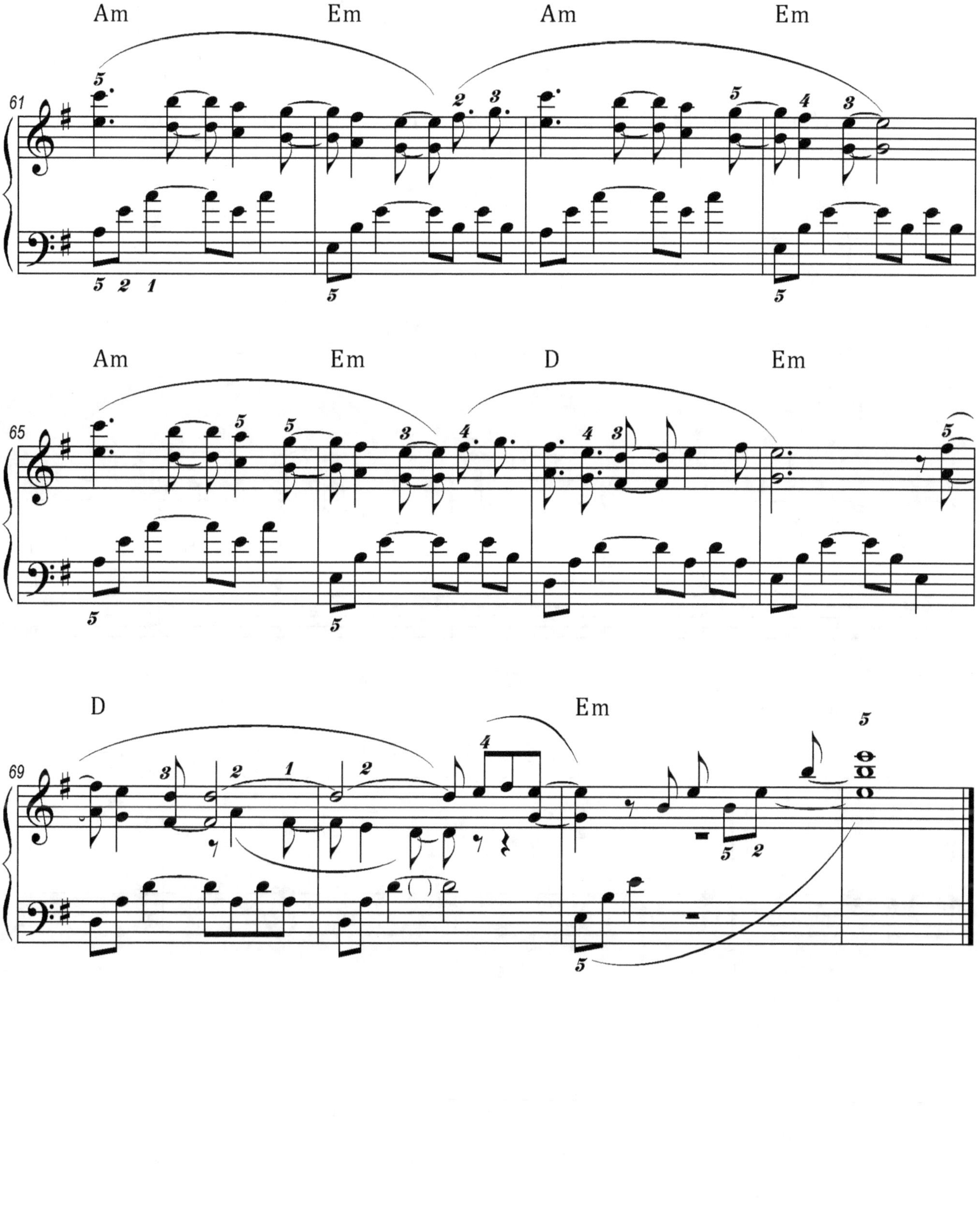
Am Em Am Em
Am Em D Em
D Em

Naomi - Fantasie
(skeleton music)

R A Chappell

G
D
Em
Am
Am6
Am
Am6
Em
Am
Am6
Am
Am6
Em
Am
Em
Am
Em
Am
Em
D
Em
D
Em
RH
LH

The Ladder

'Ladders' is a Musicarta-only term for the rising and falling musical figures which use only the root and fifth of a chord.

A lot of the pieces in this workbook use ladders as endings or between-versions fillers, but in fact, they are a good recipe for 'just sitting down and playing'. Because there are only two notes involved, ladders are a good exercise in simply getting the notes coming on time. They are also good for gently increasing the tonal 'span' of your playing, by increasing the width of keyboard you feel comfortable using.

Because the musical material stays the same, ladders also present an excellent opportunity to crescendo and diminuendo effects and rhythmic stress. Two ladders a whole tone apart – like the C and D and E and D pairs the workbook started with – are sufficient 'seed' material for extensive soundtrack-like material.

The Ladder piano solo

The piano solo *The Ladder* shows how you can create an accompaniment from ladders by simply 'changing one note' (a favourite improviser's trick). Here, the bass note of an E minor chord drops to D, C sharp and then C while the rest of the keyboard texture essentially stays in E minor. A contrasting middle section (the 'B' of the ABA structure) saves the piece from sounding repetitive.

Here are the chord sequence and the file reference numbers. Each cell in the chord sequence table represents two bars of music.

1 (Intro)

Em	Em/D	Em/C♯	Cmaj7

9 ('A' section)

Em	Em/D	Em/C♯	Cmaj7	Em	Em/D	Em/C♯	Cmaj7

25 ('B' section)

Am7 : B7	Em /D : Em/C♯	Cmaj7 : Am6	F♯m7♭5 : B7

33 ('A' section)

Em	Em/D	Em/C♯	Cmaj7	Em	Em/D	Em/C♯	Cmaj7

The Ladder perf	(Video)

You have to keep the right hand quite flat and play with straight fingers to allow the left-hand solo 'ladder' to pass over it. Unplayable or clashing 'ladder' notes are simply dropped – there's plenty happening for the ears not to notice. Watch the video to see how the hands or either over (*sopra*) or under.

The piece doesn't end on its starting chord, so it would do well as the first of a pair or little suite of repertoire performance pieces. Less experienced pianists can play the B section melody much less *rubato* without spoiling the performance.

The Ladder

R A Chappell

Em
Em/D
17
Em/C♯
Cmaj7
21
Am7
B7
Em
Em/D
Em/C
25
C
Am6
F♯m7♭5
B7
29
poco rall.

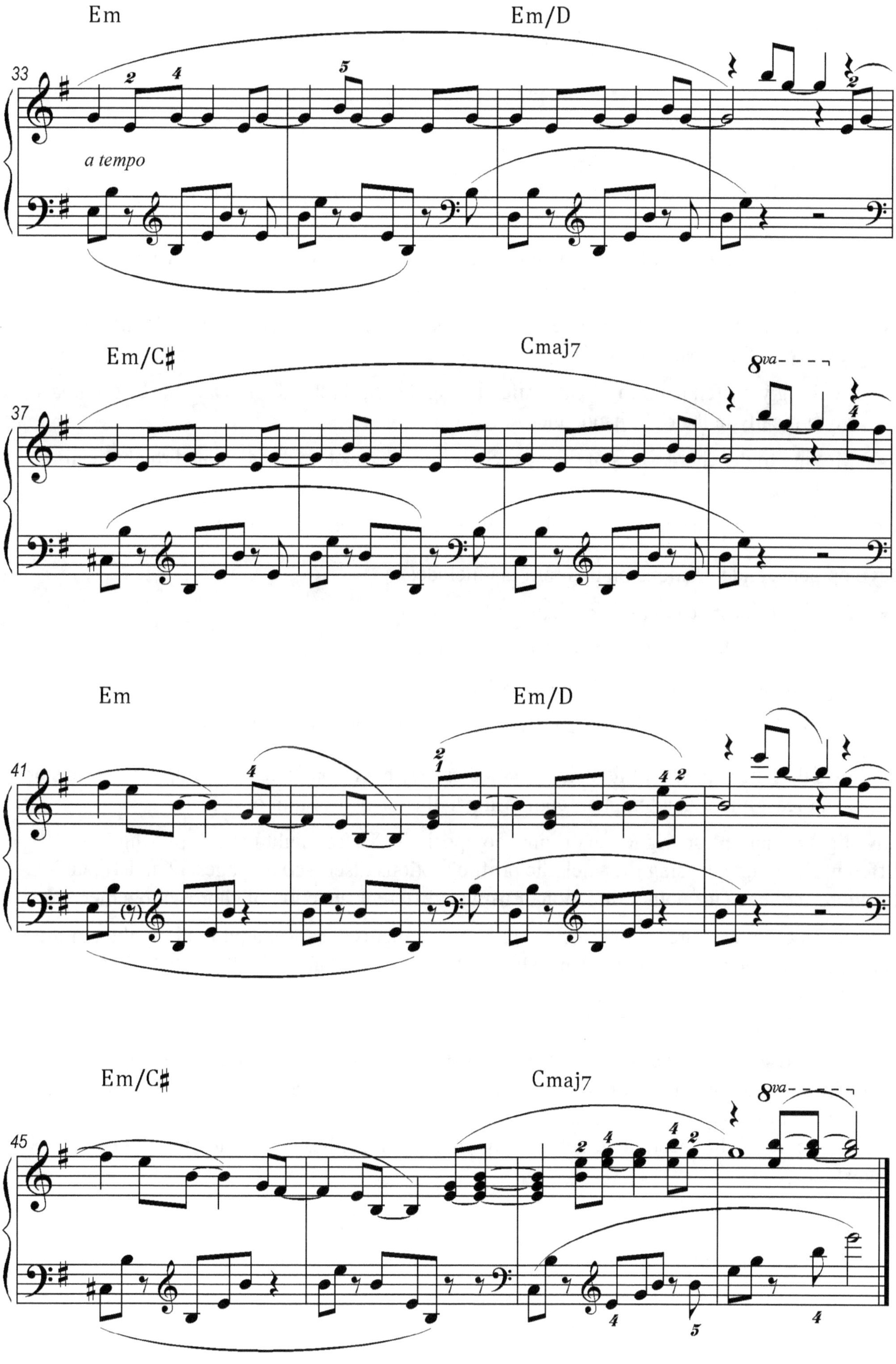
Em
Em/D
33
a tempo
Em/C♯
Cmaj7
8va
37
Em
Em/D
41
Em/C♯
Cmaj7
8va
45

Postscript

The Musicarta Easy Piano Style (MEPS) is a way of making music at the keyboard 'from scratch' – finding notes which you can be sure will sound good together and playing them in a modern syncopated way.

The MEPS workbook modules have in most cases outlined the actual process by which the module studies and pieces were composed. This MEPS process involves:

- Identifying the root, fifth, octave and third chord tones of a limited and well-patterned selection of chords;
- Rocking your left hand to a beat while playing the third (chord tone) and next-door notes rhythmically in the right hand, and/or
- Moving to the chord tones of the next chord in a pleasant, methodical and rhythmically interesting way.

(Root-and-fifth only 'ladders' are another MEPS staple content generator.)

Developments and variations on this formula include:

- Left hand 'dropped quaver' variations;
- Distributing the main four tones two-two instead of three-one;
- Right hand harmonising with thirds and sixths; and
- 'Slash chords', where the lowest note is a note other than the root of the chord.

It follows that the student of this volume, whether they have completed the course of lessons or not, can at least make an attempt at 'composing at the keyboard' him or herself.

Any slight variation can trigger an original composition. These might include playing in a different rhythm, exercising the 'melodic profile' options discussed on pages 32 and 48, taking the chord sequence in another direction or using a different selection of chords altogether.

Seeds for these adventures can be the module studies themselves – and particularly the build-up fragments – or the items on the second Mister Musicarta YouTube MEPS playlist. This includes archived material (mainly original versions of MEPS module studies) and other MEPS-based compositions.

This can be used as material for both memory test and play-by-ear practice. (The better you know the material, the more able you become to create similar music yourself.) As an exercise, put on one of the playlist videos and follow it at your keyboard, either from memory or because you can see how it has been put together. This suggestion applies equally to the original MEPS playlist.

Continue deepening your abilities by working on your existing MEPS repertoire.

- Work on your 'rhythmic smoothing' and apply it in your performances.
- Commit the studies and pieces to memory. The skeleton music and chord sequence charts provided are useful aids here, and can also provide a springboard for your own versions of

the material.

- Transpose the module studies into other keys using the MidiPiano 'Key' function.

  Transposing musical material into other keys is a great way not only of learning the material more thoroughly but of seeing into and understanding how it is constructed. Play the file and adjust the Key function by steps up or down until you find a pitch where there aren't too many black keys. Remember that you can slow down playback in MidiPiano, too. See the site navbar Transposing tab.

- Work at understanding the harmony of the MEPS pieces and studies better.

  The Modes tab on the home site navbar is particularly relevant, as most of the chord families used in the MEPS studies and pieces are modal. There is a Modes MMYT playlist, too.

  The Musicarta Key Chords lesson course teaches music harmony's theory of 'key' by introducing and coaching you in the families of chords you're most likely to find in popular music. Sample the content on the MMYT Key Chords playlist.

Post-MEPS, you might also like to move on to one of the other Musicarta study courses, such as the Musicarta's Pyramids Variations (which is about the same level of difficulty as MEPS) or the Canon Project, which is more difficult and has a greater music theory component. Link through to the MMYT Pyramids Variations and Canon Project playlists for a sample of the contents.

You could also consider purchasing the first Musicarta Solos album – most of which are loosely MEPS-based and have teaching notes and build-up exercises like those in this workbook. Sample the content via the home site Solos navbar tab and the Mister Musicarta YouTube Solos playlist.

Stay in touch, keep moving forward

As a self-directing musician, keeping yourself motivated and moving forward is challenging. Let Musicarta help by using the website and YouTube resources to the full, and by letting Musicarta remind you of developments and postings.

- Bookmark the Musicarta site and visit regularly.

- Get the site RSS feed for no-frills news updates.

- The RSS items are displayed on the site blog page – bookmark it for a one-stop what's new site visit.

- Announcements are also posted on the Musicarta Facebook page – like the page to stay in touch.

- Subscribe to Mister Musicarta YouTube for notification of new developments there.

Finally, the Musicarta newsletter offers a less frequent round-up of developments, and regularly contains discount codes for Musicarta publications.

Collected Video URLs

First Pair of Chords [FPOC] (C and D minor)   http://youtu.be/Pyqw6zKGbBM

    Build-up of syncopation   http://youtu.be/NeuD5mReZMk

Second Pair of Chords [SPOC] (E minor and D)   http://youtu.be/N0UrpMfPiDc

One Fourth and a Pair [OFAP] (*The Vigil*)   http://youtu.be/EFLwHFbJy6E

Three Fourths and a Pair [TFAP]   http://youtu.be/MSYt2szNE08

Three Fourths and a Pair in E minor [TFEM]   http://youtu.be/oM4LMMn9gC0

    Another E minor Variation   http://youtu.be/oM4LMMn9gC0

Introducing Thirds – Pairs of chords [ITPC] (C and D minor)   http://youtu.be/8d7f1412Ijc

Thirds – Pairs of chords [ITPC] (E minor and D)   http://youtu.be/UWx5y5V4ub8

    E minor and D - Build-up of Syncopation   http://youtu.be/cSgpv1srSwM

Archived Thirds/Pairs of Chords videos

    C and D minor   http://youtu.be/FooZjLM4SN0

    E minor and D   http://youtu.be/QExZ88QJPl8

Exercises for Thirds [EX3]   (see MMYT Technical Exercises playlist)

Tanza   http://youtu.be/ocGekyV6WUI

Afternoon   http://youtu.be/kSw_FRRSnMU

Ever True   http://youtu.be/cX0c_ZgxldE

Fanfare   http://youtu.be/9szkkMX9K-k

An Unsettling Notion   http://youtu.be/Hi1Nn_L_y-A

Introducing Sixths – One Fourth in Sixths [OFIS]   http://youtu.be/kBs9JghzheQ

Three Fourths in Sixths [TFIS]   http://youtu.be/C8pWOUrf5Eg

Exercises for Sixths [EX6]   http://youtu.be/zusy8H7WUgA

Sixths Study – MEPS Diary 29-06-13 (*A Dilemma*) [SIST]   http://youtu.be/r_Nro-FCgbg

    MEPS 29-06-13 Syncopation Drill   http://youtu.be/fVBTn5IilTY

Sixths Riff – MEPS Diary 12-11-13 [SIRI]   http://youtu.be/LtaA2nRhY08

Tanza revisited   http://youtu.be/ZB5IYJU1200

Naomi - Fantasie   http://youtu.be/J1d66AOb6wU

The Ladder   http://youtu.be/T0T52J6W-yI

Musicarta MEPS home page   http://www.musicarta.com/MEPS_home.html

Mister Musicarta YouTube MEPS playlist   MMYT MEPS playlist

MMYT MEPS Playlist 2   MMYT MEPS Playlist 2

Exercises for Thirds and Sixths

Thirds and sixths are the harmonious intervals – they sound good moving in parallel, and offer an easy way to harmonise a tune in the right hand. Modern-styles keyboard players should work at the ability to find and play running thirds and sixths in the right hand.

The MS for the thirds and sixths exercises is on the following pages. The accompanying videos and MIDI files are as follows.

Exercises for Thirds

EX3_01	Set One		EX3_02	Set Two		EX3_03	Set Three

EX3_04	Set Four		EX3_05	Set Five

Exercises for Sixths

EX6_01	MMYT

Exercises for Thirds

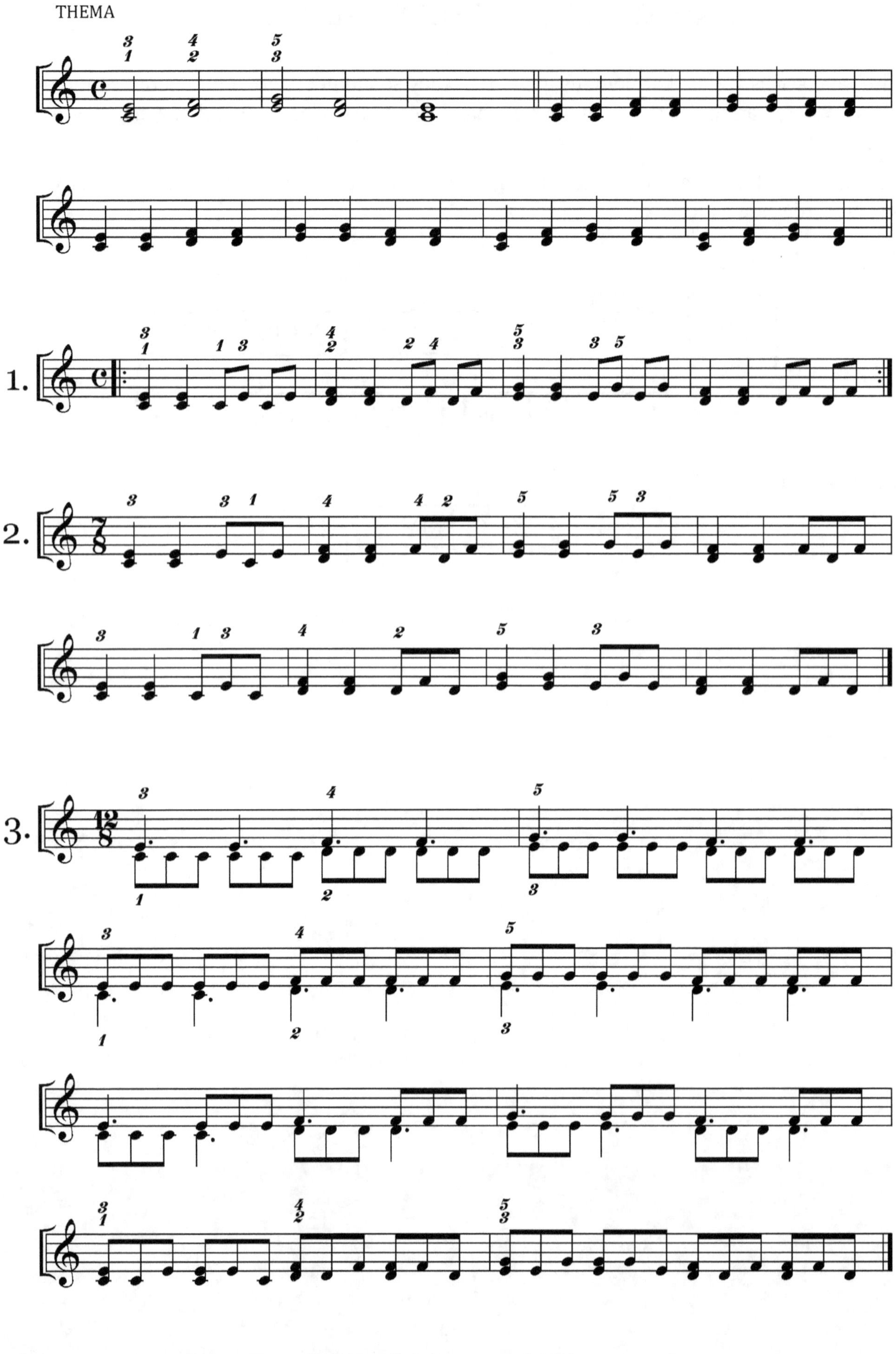

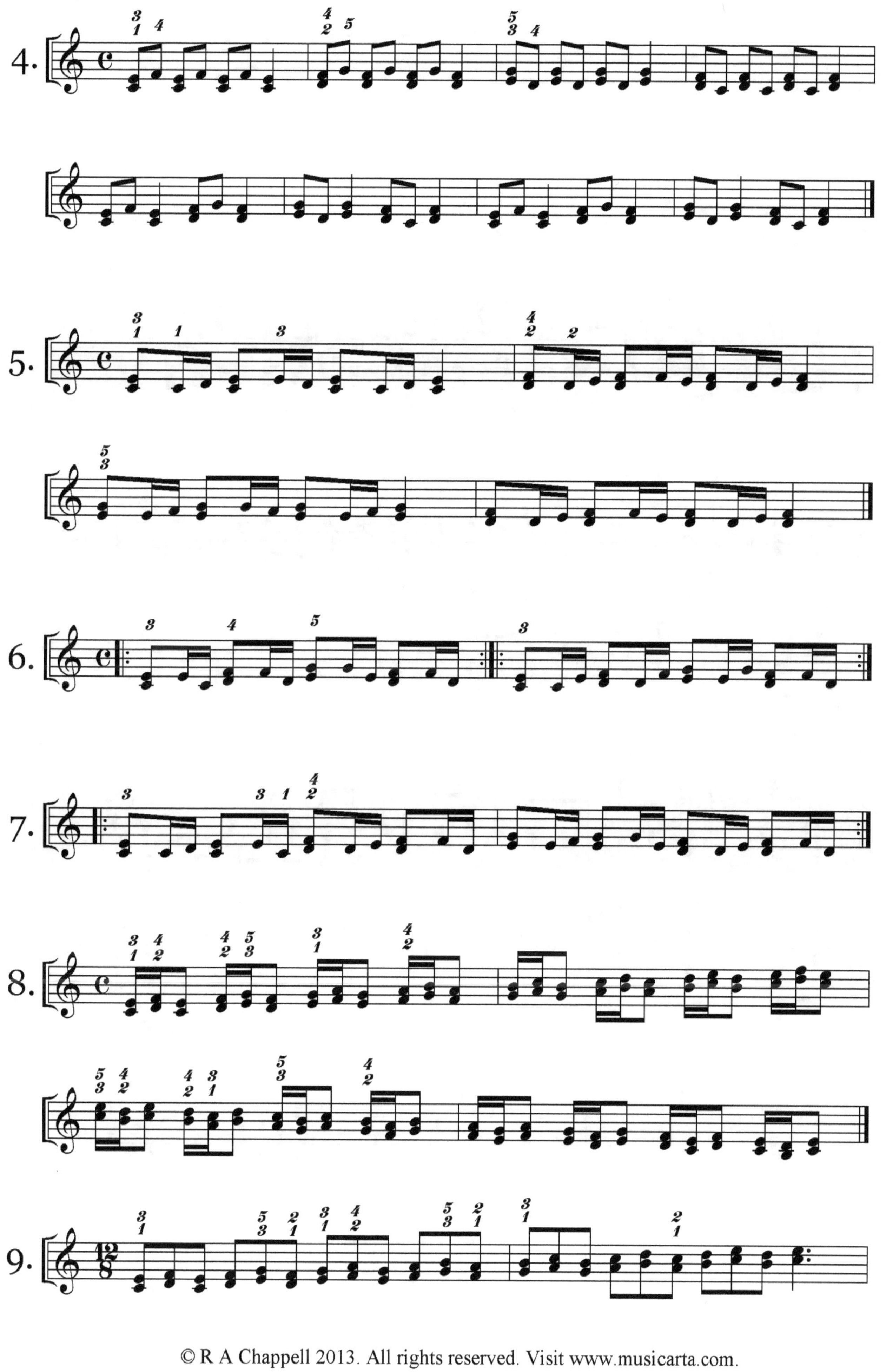
4.
5.
6.
7.
8.
9.

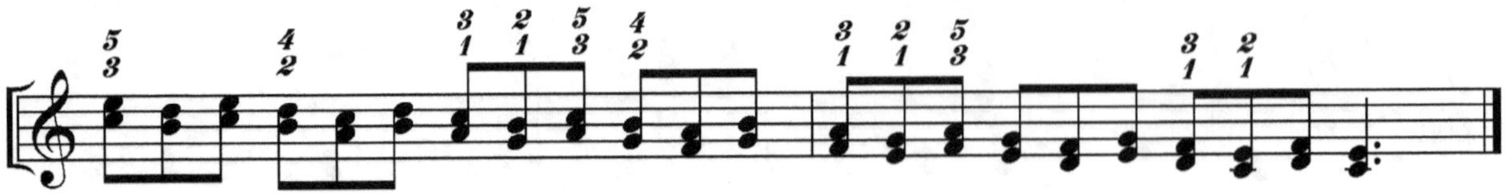

10.

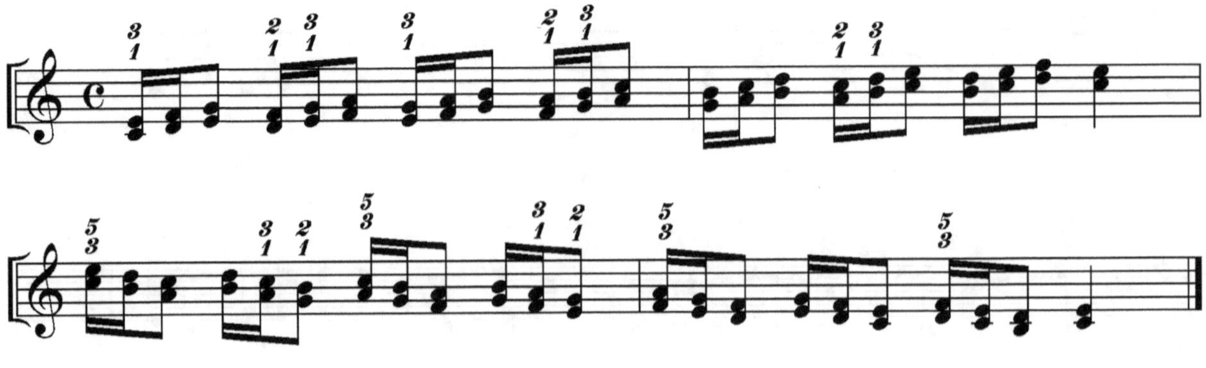

11.

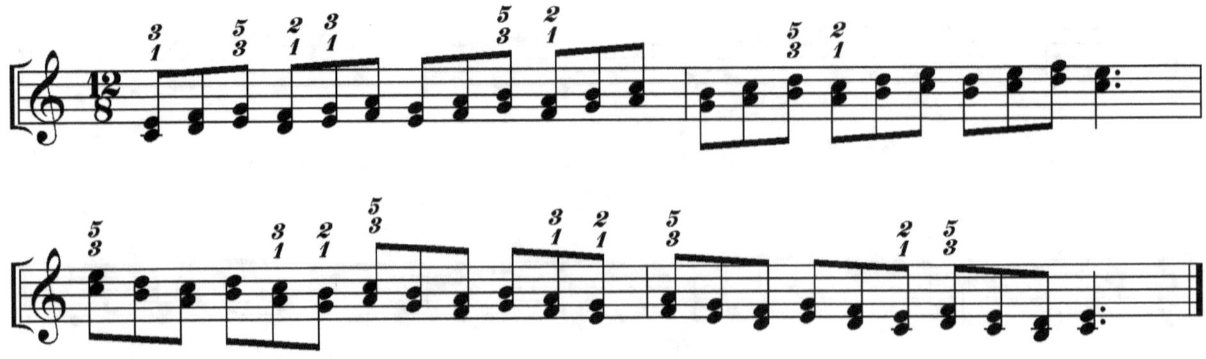

12.

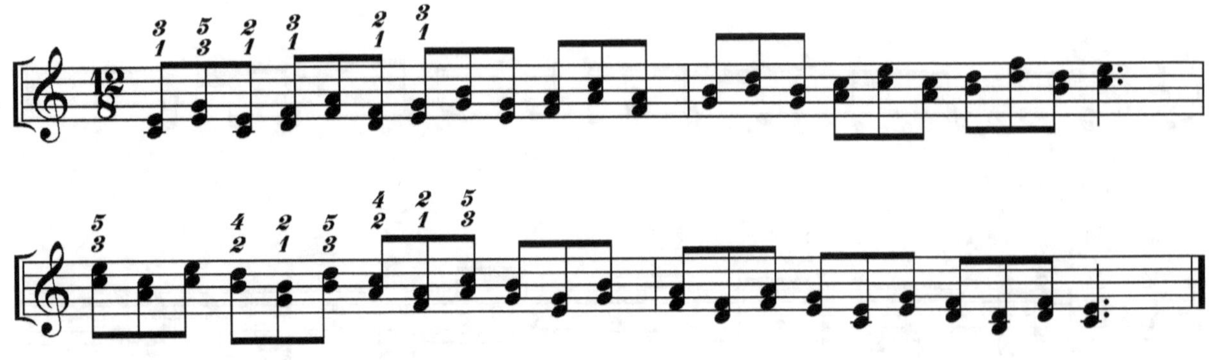

13.

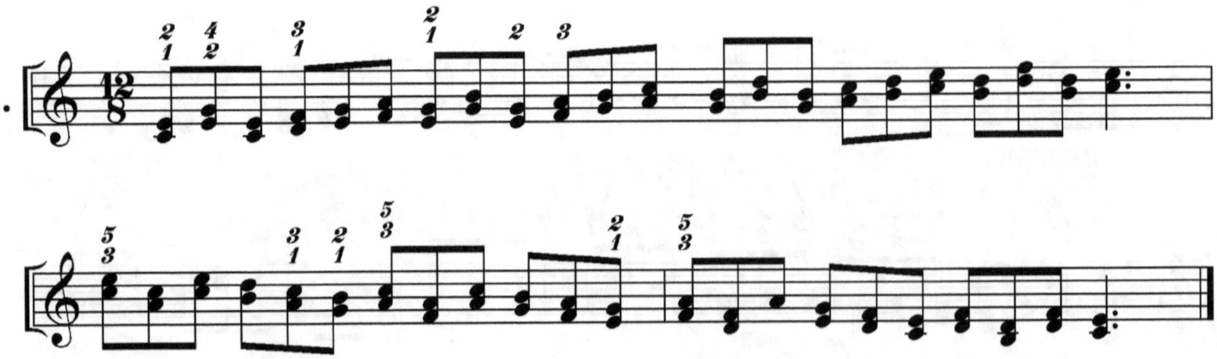

14.

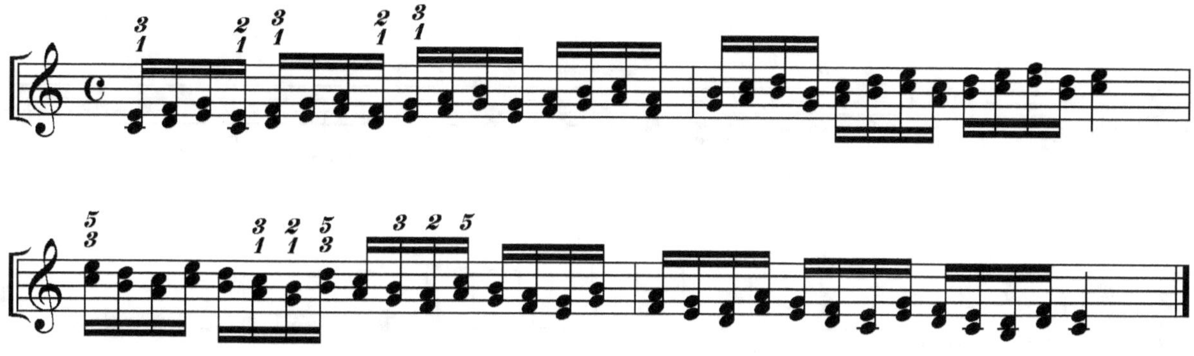

15.

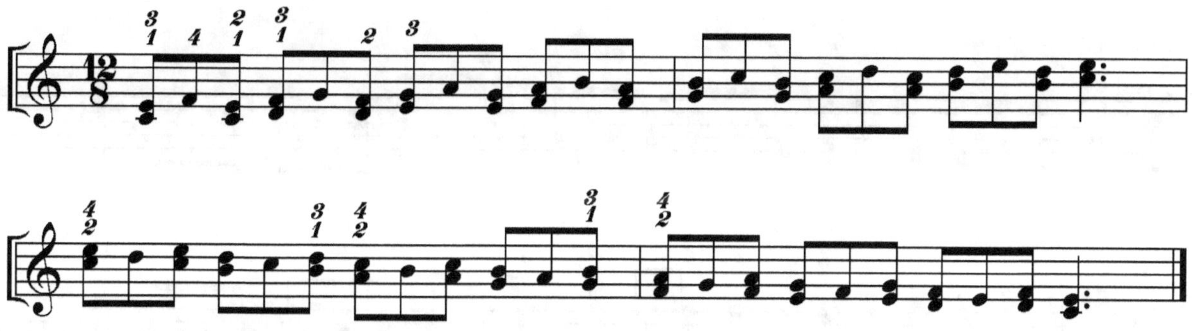

16.

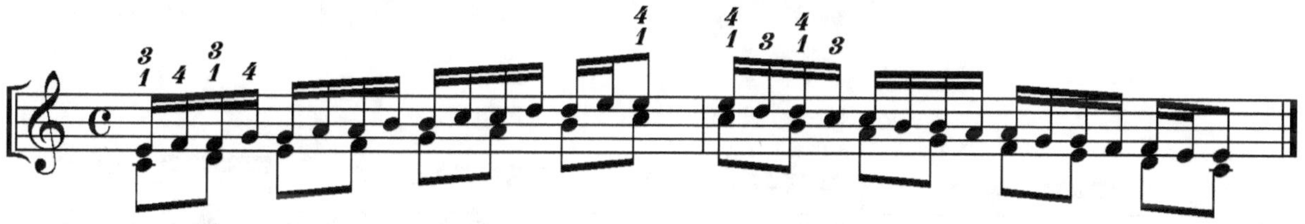

17.

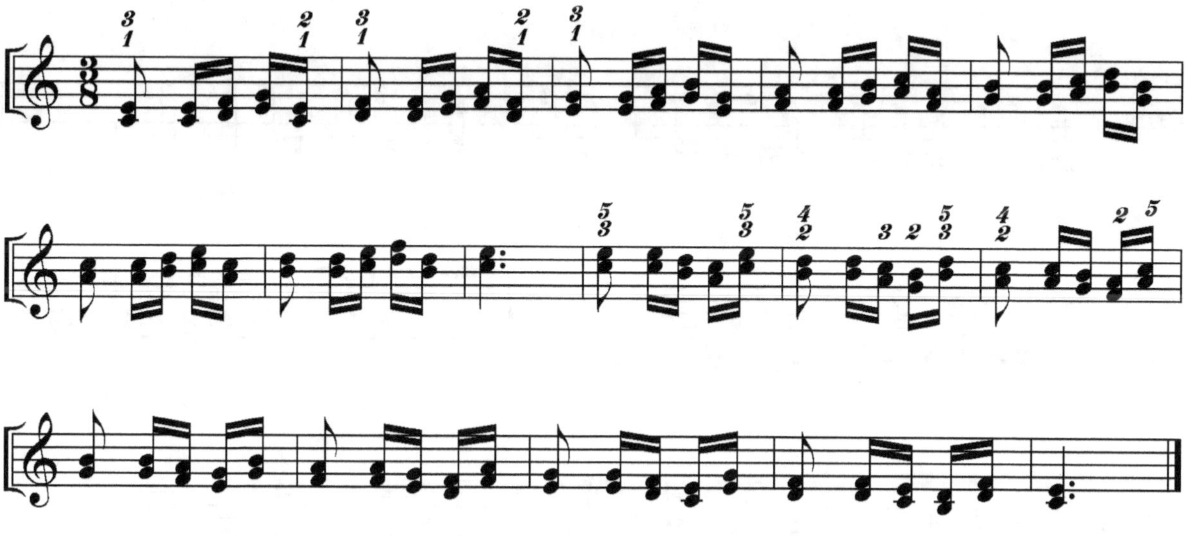

18.

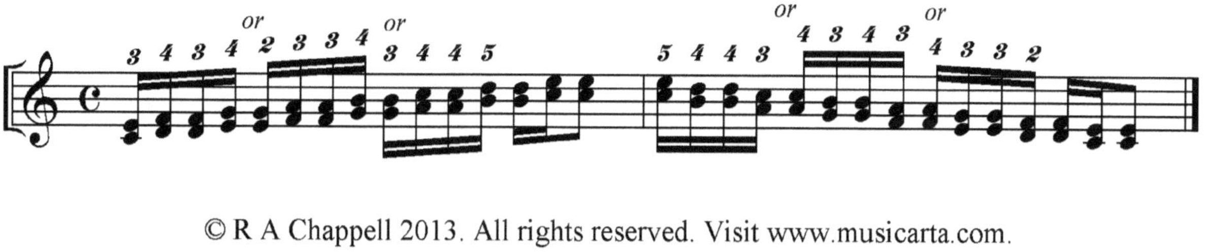

19.

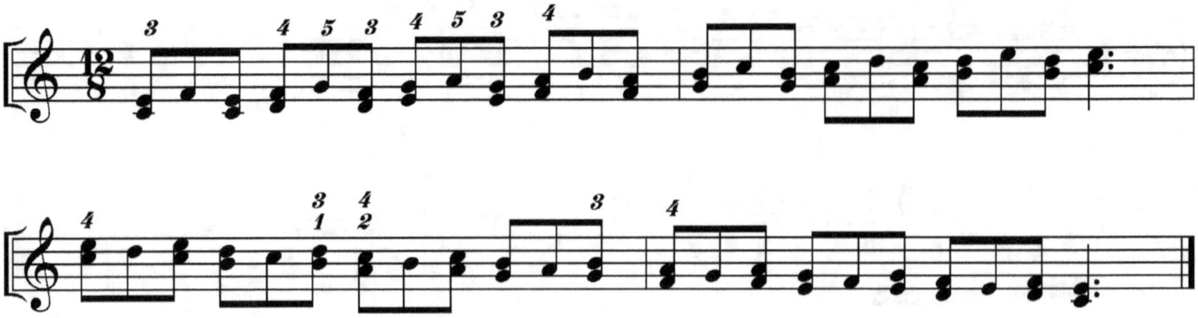

20.

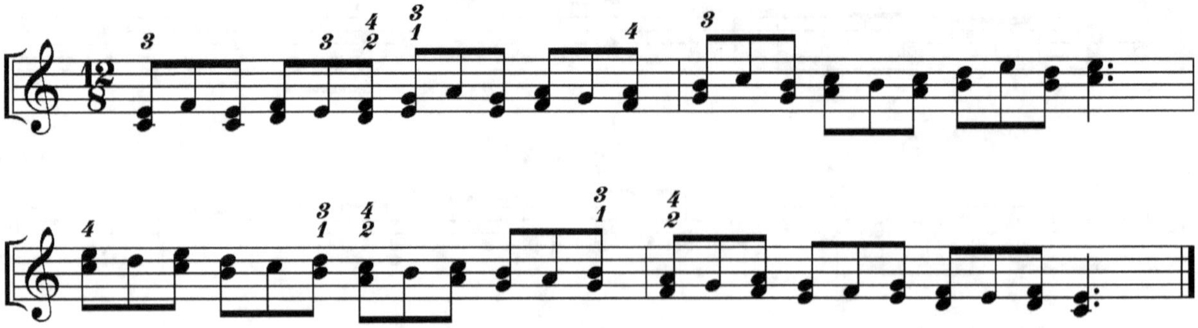

21.

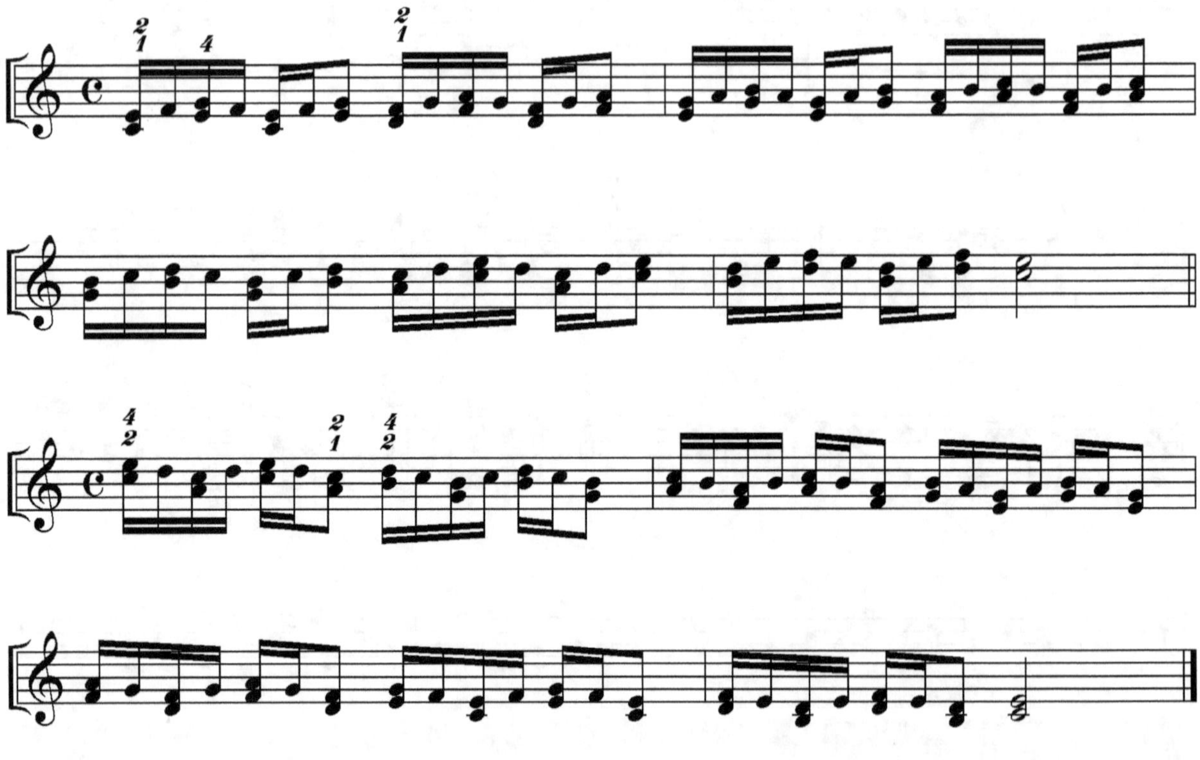

Exercises for Sixths

5.

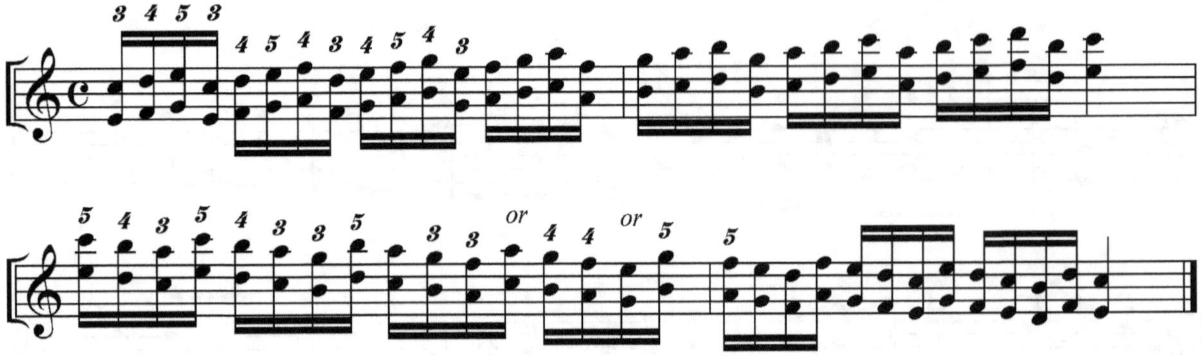

6.

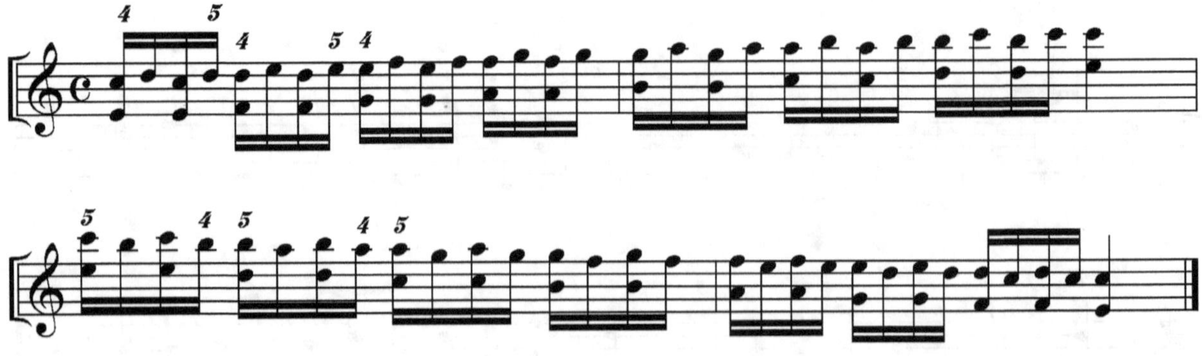

7.

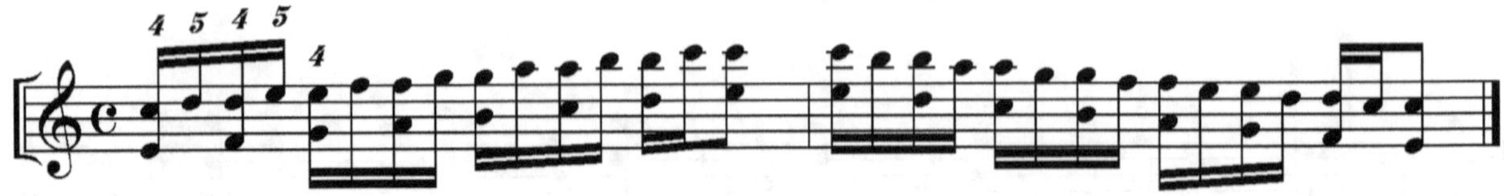

8.

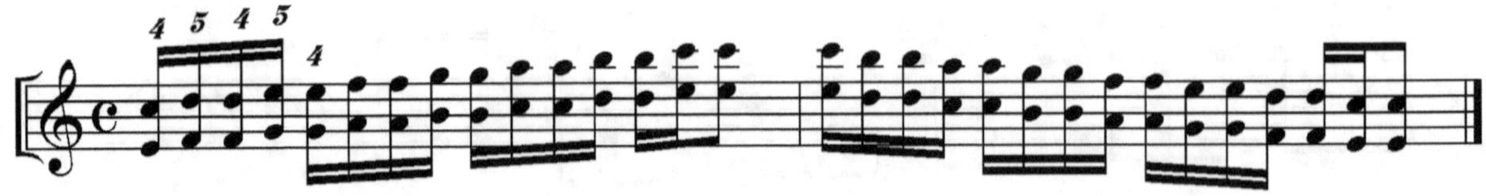

9.

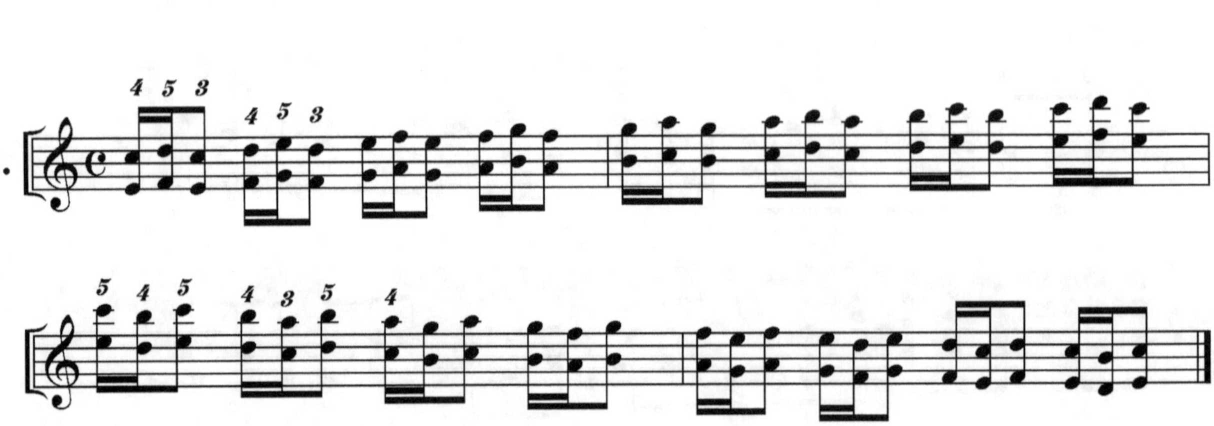

10.

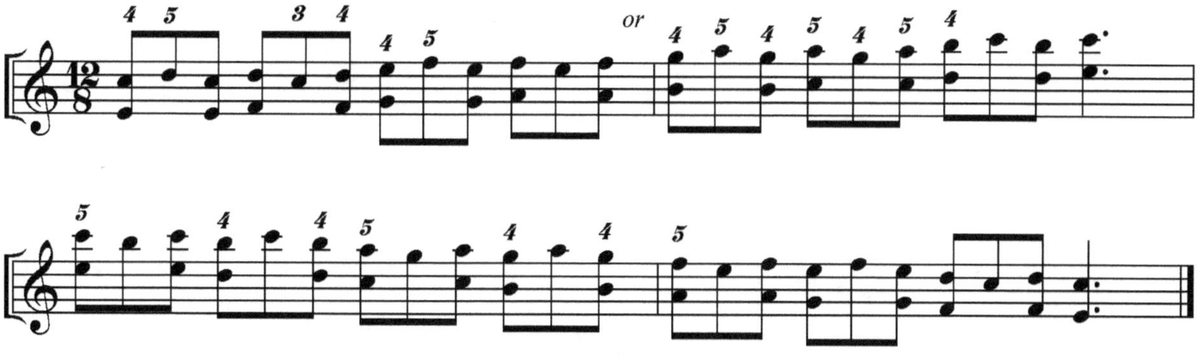

11.

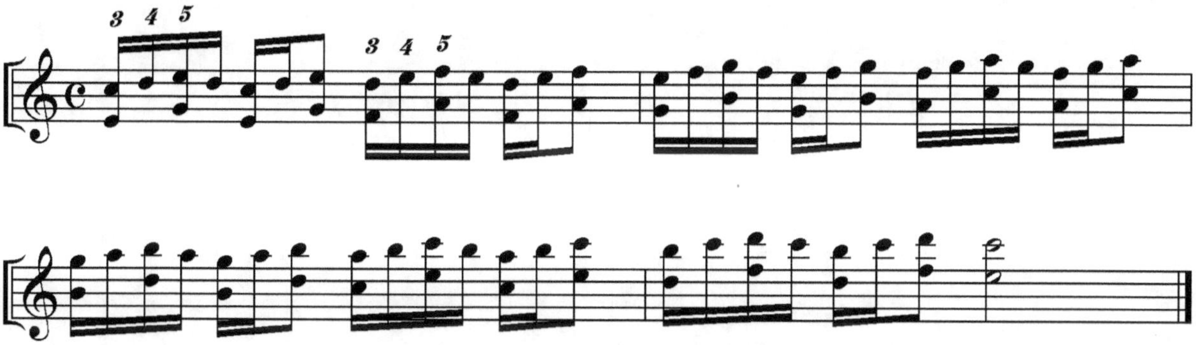

12.

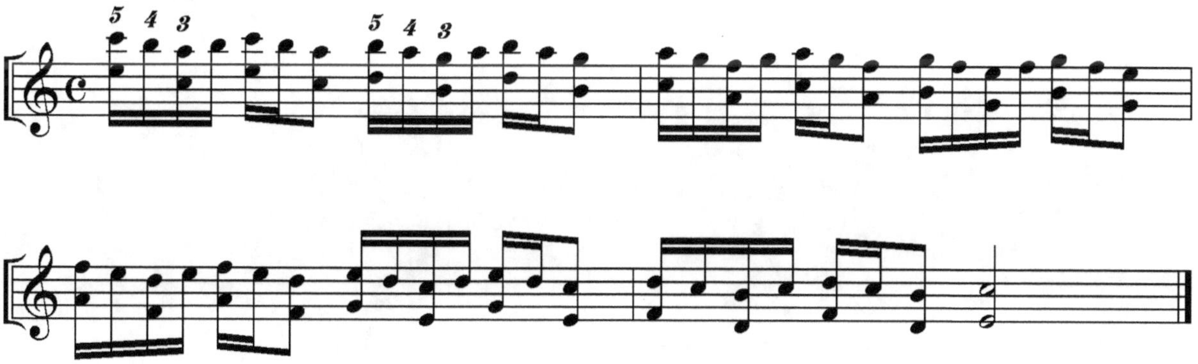

13.

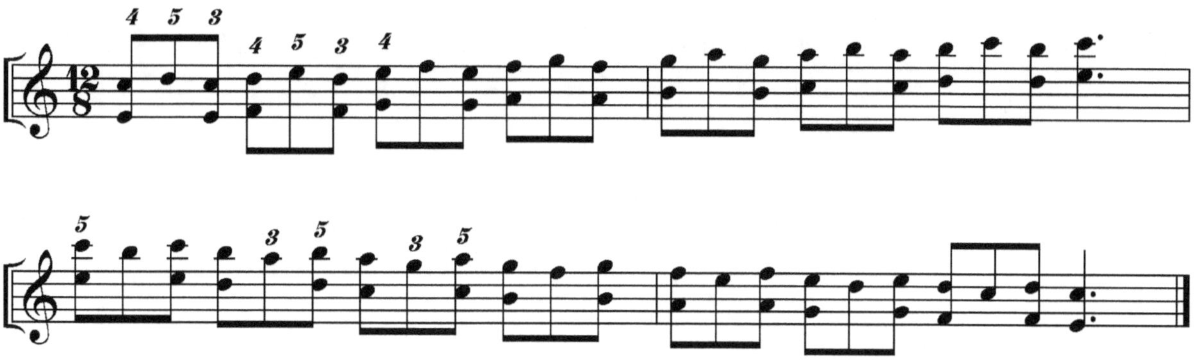